Alastair Sawday's

Special Places to Stay

Devon & Cornwall

First edition

Published in 2008

Alastair Sawday Publishing Co. Ltd,
The Old Farmyard, Yanley Lane,
Long Ashton, Bristol BS41 9LR, UK
Tel: +44 (0)1275 395430
Fax: +44 (0)1275 393388
Email: info@sawdays.co.uk
Web: www.sawdays.co.uk

The Globe Pequot Press,
P. O. Box 480, Guilford,
Connecticut 06437, USA
Tel: +1 203 458 4500
Fax: +1 203 458 4601
Email: info@globepequot.com
Web: www.globepequot.com

Design concept: Company X, Bristol
Maps: Maidenhead Cartographic Services
Printing: Butler & Tanner, Frome
UK distribution: Penguin UK, London

ISBN-13: 978-1-906136-01-7

A catalogue record for this book is available from the British Library.

Cover design: Company X, Bristol.
Cover photo credits. Thanks to: 1. Peter Adams/Getty
2. Karyn Millet/Redcover.com 3. Quentin Craven
Photo right: www.istockphotos.com

Contents

Introduction 4

How do we choose our Special Places? 7

- Inspections 7
- Feedback 7
- Subscriptions 8
- Disclaimer 8

Using this book 9

- Finding the right place for you 9
- Maps 10
- Symbols 10
- Quick reference indices 10

Practical matters 11

- Rooms 11
- Meals 11
- Bookings and cancellations 11
- Payment 11

Go Slow in Devon and Cornwall 12

The best beaches 16

Cream teas 21

Walking and nature 25

Pubs and inns 29

Wet days out with kids 35

Outdoor adventures 40

Maps 44

Guide entries 50

Feedback form 229

Quick reference indices 232

- Wheelchair-accessible 232
- WiFi 232
- National Cycle Network 232

Index by property name 234

Index by town 238

What's in each entry 240

"Let's motor down to Cornwall," said my father in 1962. We lived in Northumberland, so the journey took eight hours, excruciatingly long for a six-year-old stuck in the back with a brother whose idea of fun was to randomly apply Chinese burns. But all was forgotten on arrival, and I thought we had come to a foreign country. Palm trees! Hot sunshine! Blue sea!

This wasn't the green sea of Holy Island, or the grey sea of Bamburgh. This wasn't endless dunes towered over by medieval castles, with grasses sharp enough to cut a small foot off. I had never sat on a beach without a windbreak, never worn a swimsuit without a jumper on top, never experienced pushing my limbs down into sand that was warm, never walked into the sea without screaming and running straight back out. Best of all, in my opinion, there were 'facilities' – little cafes, shops selling buckets and spades, ice cream vans, even proper car parks that my Dad grudgingly had to pay for, so old-fashioned thriftiness dictated we stayed all day. I thought I had gone to heaven.

Years later, when I discovered Devon, it was Dartmoor that I fell in love with. Thrilled and exhilarated by the rugged bleakness of the higher parts with their thick coats of bracken and heather, the uninterrupted remoteness and the lack of noise, the grim granite eruptions, the chomping, wild-eyed ponies, I was seduced immediately. It is the sheer diversity of these western outposts that continues to lure holiday-makers, artists, surfers and old-timers looking for a bit of peace. There's no better place to bowl down an emerald-fringed narrow road and arrive at the

Photo right: Southcliffe Hall, entry 74
Photo left: Tor Cottage, entry 60

sparkling coast, be pummelled by wild waves and crashing breakers, then half a mile inland have a cream tea outside a thatched cottage with not a hint of a breeze. Where else can you walk the stunning coastal path, up and down for miles, and, just when your water is running out and you've given up hope of seeing civilisation, find a working fishing village with a pub selling fresh crab sandwiches and real ale? You can be dazzled by art and sculpture in a space that overlooks a perfect milky sky and curved sandy bay, or sit outdoors to watch worthy thespians strut their stuff by moonlight, splash out on trendy restaurants or just stay outdoors and sizzle the mackerel you've caught that day.

In this new pocket-sized book you will find places to stay that are just as varied, delightfully different. Here is a rich mix of beautiful B&Bs, charming hotels, lively inns and self-catering cottages from swish to rustic, so you can unearth the treasures of both counties in your own way, at your own pace. There are also some pages devoted to suggestions for walks, beaches, cream teas and how to entertain children on a wet day; no excuse for turning on the television or wondering what to do next. Open yourself up to the joys of Devon and Cornwall and allow yourself to be led astray. You may never want to stand in an airport queue again.

Nicola Crosse

Photo: Higher Wiscombe, entry 6

It's simple. There are no rules, no boxes to tick. We choose places that we like. We also recognise that one person's idea of special is not necessarily someone else's so we try to give a variety of places, and prices. We take huge pleasure in finding people and places that do their own thing – brilliantly; places that are unusual and follow no trends; places of peace and beauty; people who are kind and interesting – and genuine.

Unearth the treasures of both counties in your own way, at your own pace

Inspections

We visit every place to get a feel for how it ticks. We don't take a clipboard and we don't have a list of what is acceptable and what is not. Instead, we chat for an hour or so with the owner or manager and then look round. It's all very informal, but it gives us an excellent idea of who would enjoy staying there. If the visit happens to be the last of the day, we sometimes stay the night. Places are then revisited regularly so that we can keep things fresh and up to date.

Feedback

In between inspections we rely on feedback from our readers, as well as from staff members who are encouraged to visit places across the series. This feedback is invaluable and we always follow up on comments. We like your recommendations, too. So please stay in touch and tell us about your experiences and your discoveries. You can use the feedback form in this book or on our website at www.sawdays.co.uk.

Photo: West Charleton Grange, entry 50

Occasionally misunderstandings occur, even with the best of intentions. So if your bedroom is cold or the bedside light is broken, please don't seethe silently and write to us a week later. Say something to the owners at the time. They will be keen to put things right if they can.

Subscriptions

Owners pay to appear in our guides. Their fees go towards the high cost of inspections, of producing an all-colour book and of maintaining our website. We only include places and owners that we find positively special. It is not possible for anyone to buy their way into our guides.

Disclaimer

We make no claims to pure objectivity in choosing our Special Places. They are here because we like them. Our opinions and tastes are ours alone and this book is a statement of them; we hope that you will share them. We have done our utmost to get our facts right but apologise unreservedly for any mistakes that may have crept in.

You should know that we do not check such things as fire alarms, swimming pool security or any other regulation with which owners of properties receiving paying guests should comply. This is the responsibility of the owners.

Photo: Lewtrenchard Manor, entry 63

Finding the right place for you

Our descriptions are carefully written to help you steer clear of places that will not suit you, but lead you instead to personal paradise. So read between the lines: what we don't say is sometimes as important as what we do.

Wherever you choose to stay, remember that the owners are experts at knowing their patch. They can often recommend secret beaches, quaint tea rooms, super walks and gardens to visit – occasionally ones that aren't usually open to the public. Some places may provide maps and a bus timetable; some owners may be happy to pick you up at the end of a long walk. Do ask.

On the B&B pages you will find a huge variety of places, and also owners: some will be hovering with freshly baked cake when you arrive, others may be out shopping for your supper, having left a key under a stone. Mostly these are people's homes; you will encounter family life and its attendant chaos in some, and complete privacy in others, while a fair number of owners will be happy for you to stay all day.

Photo: The Old Quay House Hotel, entry 159

For those who prefer more anonymity, there are some wonderful hotels and inns to choose from, some particularly child-friendly, others more suited to romantic couples or those who prefer peace and quiet. A sprinkling of deeply spoiling and more expensive hotels will keep the fashionistas happy, while there are some small, family-run, and comfortingly old-fashioned places for traditionalists. There are also some gorgeous self-catering places, from crisply chic to simple but cosy. Sometimes these are run alongside a B&B – thus perfect for family gatherings and big parties.

Maps

Each property is flagged with its entry number on the maps at the front. These maps are the best start to planning your trip, but you'll need a proper road map for real navigation. Most places will send you detailed instructions once you have booked your stay.

We take huge pleasure in finding people and places that do their own thing – brilliantly

Symbols

Below each entry you will see some little symbols, which are explained in a short table at the very back of the book. They are based on information given to us by owners. However, things do change: bikes may be under repair or a new pool may have been put in. Please use the symbols as a guide rather than an absolute statement of fact. Owners occasionally bend their own rules, so it is worth asking if you may take your child or dog, even if the entry doesn't have the symbol.

Children – The symbol is given to owners who accept children of any age. It does not mean they will necessarily have cots, highchairs, safety equipment etc, so do check. If an owner welcomes children but only those above a certain age, this is stated at the end of the description. Even these folk may accept your younger child if you are the only guests. Many who say no to children do so not because they don't like them but because they may have a steep stair, an unfenced pond or they find balancing the needs of mixed age groups too challenging.

Pets – The symbol is given to places where your pet can sleep in your bedroom but not on the bed. Be realistic about your pet – if it is nervous or excitable or doesn't like the company of other dogs, people, chickens or children, then say so.

Quick reference indices

At the back of the book (page 232) we list those places:

- suitable for wheelchair users
- with wireless internet access available
- within 2 miles of a National Cycle Network route.

Rooms

Bedrooms – We tell you if a room is a double, twin/double (ie. with zip and link beds), suite (with a sitting area), family or single. Most owners are flexible and can often juggle beds or bedrooms; talk to them about what you need before you book. Most bedrooms in this book have an en suite bath or shower room; we only mention bathroom details when they do not.

Meals

In B&Bs, hotels and inns, unless we say otherwise, a full cooked breakfast is included. Apart from breakfast, no meals should be expected unless you have arranged them in advance. Obviously if you have chosen to self-cater, you must organise your own breakfast.

Bookings and cancellations

Requests for deposits vary; some are non-refundable, and some owners may charge you for the whole of the booked stay in advance.

Some cancellation policies are also more stringent than others. Some will charge you the total cost if you cancel at short notice. If they hold your credit card details they may deduct a cancellation fee from it and not contact you to discuss this. So ask owners to explain their cancellation policy clearly before booking so you understand exactly where you stand; it may well help you avoid a nasty surprise.

Photo: Beachmodern No. 28, entry 89

Payment

All our owners take cash and UK cheques with a cheque card. Those who also take credit cards have the appropriate symbol.

Do remember that this book lasts for two years, so during its lifetime prices may go up.

What is the Slow Movement really about? Most people know of the Slow Food movement and its determination to oppose the culture of fast food, and many are also aware of Cittaslow, which tries to counteract the homogenisation of our towns and cities. But there is a wider philosophy here too, as an antidote to our culture of haste, a determination to appreciate differences and a willingness to preserve our traditions. We think it is about all of these things and more.

So why go slow? According to the World Institute of Slowness, adopting a slow lifestyle will make us feel better about ourselves, save us money, improve our physical and mental health, help us to see the world as it is meant to be seen – and liven up our sex lives. So don't whip through these counties in a hurry, savour them. Here are some places where you can enjoy lovely, local and, best of all, slow experiences.

Exeter Slow Food Market Exeter (01297 442378). Held every third Saturday of the month, 10am-3pm. Wander the quayside, mosey around the stalls, then follow the canal, past Powderham Castle and fields of deer, to the Exe estuary and the riverside hamlet of Cockwood. Bring out the rug and the picnic, wash it all down with a pint at the pub.

Tavistock Markets Tavistock (www.tavistockpanniermarket.co.uk; www.tavistockfarmersmarket.com). The undercover pannier market, built in 1850, is a treasure trove of all sorts (closed Sunday and Monday). There are plenty of cafés in town for lunch and a good farmers' market in Bedford Square on the second and fourth Saturday of the month.

Lemon Street Market Truro (01872 273031). Cornwall's sole city, Truro, is a foodie hub. Visit the

Photo: Tom Germain

undercover market for fruit juices and smoothies, unusual chutneys, recycled and fair-trade goods and an art gallery. There's a really good farmers' market on Wednesdays and Saturdays, too.

Sharpham Vineyard Totnes (01803 732203; www.sharpham.com). Grapes grow on the sheltered slopes of the Dart, so wander the estate or join a tasting tour. There's cheese to buy too, from organically reared Jersey cattle, and a café.

Camel Valley Vineyard Nanstallon, Two miles from Bodmin (01208 77959; www.camelvalley.com). Come for a late afternoon tour (from April until October) or simply turn up to sample some award-winning Cornish wine on the terrace.

Countryman Cider Milton Abbot (01822 870226; www.crying-fox.com/cider1.htm). An apple mill and cider press in 15th-century stables; an orchard on the bank of the river Tamar. Bring your own containers and take some home.

Cornish Orchards Westnorth Manor Farm, Duloe (01503 269007; www.cornishorchards.co.uk). The first proper crop came in 1999; overwhelmed, and umpteen apple pies later, Cornish Orchards sprung up. Take your pick from juices, ciders and punches. If there's time, they'll introduce you to Sophia and Demelza, the capping and labelling machines.

South Devon Chilli Farm Loddiswell, nr Kingsbridge (01548 550782; www.southdevonchillifarm.co.uk). Peer down the show tunnel at 100 varieties of chillies; buy them fresh in the shop from June to November or

Photo: Quentin Craven

take home some seeds and grow your own. And don't forget to try the chilli chocolate.

Cheristow Lavender Farm (01237 440101; www.cheristow.co.uk). Come to swoon over Eric's 120 varieties of lavender, farmed under a countryside stewardship scheme. Take home some Pretty Polly, Papillon or Lilac Wings to pot up; gift soaps, oils and pouches, too, and a tea room with views and homemade puds.

River Cottage Local Produce Store & Canteen Axminster (01297 631715). On Trinity Square, the latest addition to Hugh Fearnley-Whittingstall's real food (as in organic, seasonal, local, nutritious and delicious) empire.

Otterton Mill Budleigh Salterton (01395 568521; www.ottertonmill.com). There's been a watermill at Otterton since 100AD. Come to potter around the artists' studios before lunch or dinner in the restaurant (sometimes with live music) or time your visit to coincide with milling day.

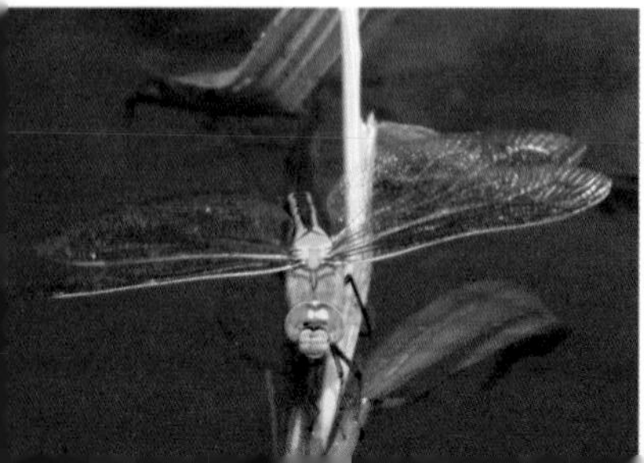

Tapeley Park Gardens Bideford (01271 860897; www.tapeleypark.com). Crumbling splendour: a lovers' evergreen tunnel with a hidden stone seat and lily-dotted lake. Tea and cakes in the old dairy and occasional 'Health and Harmony' weekends.

Tiverton Canal Company (01884 253345; www.tivertoncanal.co.uk). 'The fastest way to slow down': hop on the barge as the horse tows you along the canal path. Spot otters, dragonflies, kingfishers and swans.

Lundy Island (01271 863636; www.lundyisland.co.uk). Sail off on the MS Oldenburgh from Bideford or Ilfracombe to little Lundy: three and a half miles long, half a mile wide. Take the binoculars for guillemots, fulmars, puffins; join an organised rocky shore ramble with the warden (free).

Photo: Tom Germain

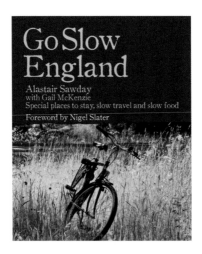

Being on a beach, staring at the sea, is wonderfully restful. You stop at last: there is no further to go. There is something about the sea, too, that is mesmerising. When it is still, cormorants spread black angel wings to air, and you're soothed; when it's angry, loose birds whirl their way up over the breakers, and it energises you.

The magical Devon and Cornwall coastline changes as you move along it and around it. Along the north coast, the Atlantic unfurls itself against massive swathes of sand, making itself irresistible to surfers, body boarders and brave souls in sea kayaks. Slip southwards and things become more serene – a smooth sea, Fresian-flecked fields, tiny smugglers' coves.

Photos: Toby Sawday

True, these far western parts can, occasionally, be a touch misty, but they're rarely really chilly so there's every reason to drop down to as many of the 400 beaches as you can, whatever the time of year. Having said that, a gorgeous time to be by the sea is spring, when the gorse is popping up all over the cliff tops – or a rogue hot day in late summer or early autumn, after August's beach tents have decamped and you can see the sand again.

Seek out a smooth rock armchair, book in hand – or slip into your swimsuit and the surf. Whatever you like to do on the beach, here are some places to inspire you.

Swimming

Bathe in safe waters at Mill Bay, in the Salcombe estuary; if you visit in high season, ferry across from Salcombe (thus avoiding limited parking at Mill Bay). You're snuggled into the estuary here, the sand is fine and there's a smattering of rock pools, too. As well as a huge beach, Summerleaze Beach (Bude) has a natural rock pool that fills at high tide, big enough to swim in, easy to reach.

Stretching the legs

The south west path covers 630 miles (the longest national trail in Britain) and the Devon and Cornwall coastline eats up a very big chunk of it. For rippling sands and gallons of sea air, park up at Saunton, then trudge the length of the beach; the further you go, the more alone you'll be. Head back through the dunes to the car park and a café with fabulous views. Or clamber over the rocks down to the sandy beach at Trebarwith Strand at high tide, and follow the coastal path to Tintagel. The views are superb.

Soft sand

Porthcurno (National Trust) at the tip of Cornwall is absolutely beautiful – broken shells in the sand give the sea a blue glaze. Gaze up west to The Minnack, an open-air theatre balanced on the cliff, or wander east to Logan Rock, a granite outcrop made famous by Lieutenant Goldsmith who tipped the eighty-ton wobbly rock at the top down, and was ordered to heave it all up again. Just out of St Ives, a good deal quieter and reachable by train, Carbis Bay has the finest sands and calmest waters: wonderful for families. At low tide, stroll across to the RSPB bird sanctuary at Porthkidney Sands.

Rock pools

Barricane Beach near Woolacombe is a little rocky cove with rock pools at low tide and shells from the Caribbean (don't take them home though). At Charleston (St Austell), the 18th-century harbour – blissfully unchanged, home to three tall ships – drops down to a shingle cove with very good rock pools. A short stroll along the coast brings you to Porthpean, sheltered and sandy with rock pools at its western tip.

Sandcastles

Bring buckets and spades to Bigbury where the water is shallow; there's a spindly-legged sea tractor that crosses to Burgh Island at high tide, and a good café, too. Porthgwidden (St Ives) is small, sheltered, lovely and it's easy to keep an eye on wandering infants. Don't miss the Moroccan-style café behind; it's child-friendly too.

Surfing

On the north coast, Croyde is a summer scramble of bucket-and-spading families and surfers, you can hire boards in the tiny thatched village and there's a surf school. The blue-flag beach of Polzeath is a fine place to sit astride a board – dolphins and seals make the occasional appearance and the tide leaves a vast pitch for beach games. For kite-surfers and land-boarders, Gwithian near Hayle has ample firm sands; at Watergate Bay there's an extreme sports academy for surfing, kite surfing, land-boarding, wave-skiing and traction kiting.

Dunes

Drift in the dunes at Braunton Burrows where rabbits scamper; it's the largest sand dune system in the UK. Visit too Penhale, Perran and Perranporth where the dunes rise up from a three-mile sweep of golden sand.

Photo: www.istockphotos.com

Barbecues

Sip while you sizzle as the sun fades. Daymer Bay, across the estuary from Padstow, looks west and is brilliant for a twilight grill; dogs can come too. Southside and shielded, the west end of the beach at Bantham has numerous sheltered nooks and crannies; gorgeous when the sun sets behind Burgh Island. (Note: the gates of the private estate close at 8.30pm, so don't bring the car in.)

Beach cafés

Flip flops are allowed at the Godrevy Café at Gwithian, a wooden chalet tucked behind dunes, with outdoor seating and scrumptious antipodean food. The Beach Restaurant at Sennen rests jammily on the cape of Cornwall: stunning views. Built by local craftsmen it has won design awards – take breakfast, brunch, lunch, tea or supper on the terrace and you'll never want to leave.

For a tea-time café in a valley, Kynance Cove is spectacular – pale sands, clear waters and caves. The Winking Prawn at North Sands, Salcombe, is a cheeky little place for sandwiches and soups, and includes a dressing up box for all ages.

Fish suppers

For a celebratory supper linger over oysters, bouillabaisse, mackerel at The Porthminster Café above the beach at St Ives. For a more sandy-toed affair, scoop up a Sri Lankan supper on the beach at The Barricane Café at Barricane Beach near Woolacombe.

Scampering dogs

When the tide's low there's a tremendous carpet of sand at Whitsand Bay; clamber down the cliff, walk for three miles. Dogs are also welcome all year round at Vault Beach near Gorran Haven: wild setting, shingley sands, calm sea. It's a fifteen-minute walk from the town. For a free leaflet on Cornish beaches that are particularly dog friendly go to www.visitcornwall.com.

Windy days

The pebbles at Beer are dotted with boats, beach huts and crab pots. The pale cliffs behind protect you on a rough day and there's a little town to wander in if a chill blows ashore. Kingsand and Cawsand are two 17th-century fishing villages that almost blend into each other, with small beaches for sailing and swimming. Warm up in the Old Boatstore Café and the Museum of Celebrity Leftovers in Kingsand, whose prize exhibit is Pete Doherty's panini crumbs… or, take the ferry to Plymouth.

Cheeky beaches

Wild Pear Beach at Coombe Martin is the one: reputedly a great spot to bare your white bits.

Kate Ball

Cream teas, cream teas? What on earth do we mean by cream teas? I once had a summer job on Dartmoor and stayed above the tea rooms of a small hotel run by my best friend's parents. Parties of American visitors would descend from coaches and swarm into the tea room kitted out in track suits, trainers and the very latest innovation, the bum bag. They were armed too with an array of umbrellas; a low and threatening cloud hung over the moor that summer. They would give the menu a cursory glance before ordering a cream tea – gee, so English, can't *wait* to try it. Half an hour later, after a great deal of clamour, the room would be empty – apart from the cups of barely sipped tea, festooned with dollops of semi-submerged clotted cream. How they must have wondered at the eccentricities of the English as they rumbled off across the moors to marvel at how we managed to ride such very small horses.

Let's start with the basics. Tea, scones, jam, cream. Ah, but there's more to it than that. Many self-respecting tea drinkers can only drink from bone china – and rightly so. The ideal cream tea comes with an elegant china tea set strewn with pink roses, loose leaf tea in a proper teapot, some extra boiling water to top it up, matching plates, a mountain of warm scones and lashings of jam and clotted cream. (Napkins wouldn't go amiss either.)

There is a debate about the correct way to eat a cream tea. Should it be served with a slice of cake? Are fruit scones

Photo: Trevor Burrows © Cornwall Tourist Board

allowed? Most controversial of all – is it jam on cream or cream on jam? The first two questions are easy enough to answer: no and no. (Although on second thoughts, why turn down a perfectly good slice of cake just to be traditional?) The third needs some serious investigation.

If you're in Cornwall, you would first spread your horizontally-split scone with butter, then strawberry jam, and then smother it in cream. If in Devon, oddly enough, it would be the opposite – but you wouldn't bother with the butter. There doesn't seem to be a particular reason for this contrary county behaviour – just jammy mindedness. I prefer the Cornish method because I can really pile on the cream without having to worry about balancing the jam on top; and let us not forget that consuming vast amounts of ticker-stopping clotted cream is one of the prime aims of the exercise. There are no half measures in this game so don't even bother ordering if you feel the need to ask for wheat-free, sugar-free or dairy-free. Just ask for a nice cup of green tea and have done.

Another anomaly is that, traditionally, the Cornish tea came with splits instead of scones. A split is a kind of sweet bread roll, which was cut in half (or should I say split) and sandwiched back together with the jam and cream. I'm not sure I like the sound of that though – I would feel slightly put out if I pitched up for my one and only cream tea of the summer and got a roll.

This might just be me but I really only enjoy the first cream tea of the year. A bit like with Pimm's – glorious the first

Photos: www.istockphotos.com

time, but rather too much of a good thing the second. So when do I feel the annual urge coming on? It has to be sunny, I have to be within two miles of the coast and it has to be at least three hours after my pasty lunch. And I would prefer to be sitting outside, even though I may have to defend the jam from a wasp invasion.

It is possible, of course, to construct your own cream tea at home, providing you have access to clotted cream or your own herd of dairy cows. If you do have a few hanging around, you milk them, heat the unpasteurised milk in a wide shallow pan, leave it until the 'clots' rise to the surface and then skim off – clotted cream! Scones are really easy too and should only take twenty minutes from start to finish – plus two minutes eating time. Or you could save yourself all the bother by ordering a mail order tea at www.seriously-good.co.uk. But let's face it, if you're reading this you'll probably be planning a trip to Devon or Cornwall and you'll be wanting to know the best places to go when you get there. So here are some ideas from those in the know: the owners of our Special Places.

Dart Valley Steam Railway (01364 642338). Sophie and Nick Colley of Tudor House recommend taking tea on a Sunday afternoon, chugging through south Devon in a vintage carriage and being served by two delightful ladies in blouses and brooches. Teas are served on Sunday afternoons from May to the end of October, for a very reasonable £3.85 plus the cost of the journey.

Stoke Barton Tearooms Hartland Quay (01237 441238). Ann and Richard Dorsett of Beara Farmhouse love these tearooms for their very fine scones and superior cakes. Closed Mondays and Fridays. Cost: £4.50 – or £5.60 if you'd rather share a tea.

Otterton Mill near Budleigh Salterton (01395 567041). Jacalyn Cole of Rose Cottage and Frank Hayes of West Colwell Farm both nominate this one. It has a wonderful laid-back atmosphere with tables next to the stream and, here's one-upmanship for you, they mill their own flour for the scones. Cost: £4.50.

The Thurlestone Hotel near Salcombe (01548 560382). We're unused to recommending hotels that aren't in our guides but cream tea on the terrace here, overlooking the sea, is a must according to Elizabeth Hanson of Rafters, Penny Cadogan of Washbrook Barn, and Maureen Ewen of Orchard Cottage – so it's got to be good. £6.25 per person and teas are served from 3pm to 5.30pm. No need to book.

Melinsey Mill Veryan. Bridget Reid of Pelyn and Clare Holdsworth of Pine Cottage recommend these very generous teas in a lush valley; open during the season only.

Cream Teas at Eglos Farm Ruan Minor. Sandy Pulfrey of The Hen House tells us that Sue's cream teas are excellent value, served on check tablecloths and surrounded by lush, green fields munched by their own dairy herd.

Porthminster Café St Ives (01736 795352). Malcolm Herring of the Blue Hayes Hotel thinks that tea here is pretty perfect with its beachside setting. So good in fact that he recommends having a lazy lunch and then staying on for scones. Open 3pm to 5pm. Cost: £4.50.

Sarah Bolton

There is a walk to suit every pair of legs in Devon and Cornwall. The rugged coastal path which follows the peninsula from Minehead in Somerset all the way round to Poole in Dorset is a challenge to the most developed of calf muscles, even in short sections, while the inland walks on the flat, around reservoirs and lakes, are ideal for the less energetic. For the averagely sporty there are walks through woodland and down pretty country lanes, across wild moors and windswept hills.

The coastal path, first conceived in the 1940s, is now 630 miles long – with a few gaps – and much of it is on land belonging to The National Trust, so it's well maintained and sign posted. The South West Coast Path Association (www.swcp.org.uk) publish an annual guide which also includes tide tables, handy for the ferry crossings necessary on some stretches.

Walking round the edge of land and looking out to sea is one of the best ways to see wildlife, especially birds. The Cornish national bird – the chough – was thought to have been extinct for fifty years, until a pair turned up on the coast of the Lizard peninsula in 2001. A member of the crow family, the chough is black with scarlet legs and beak and a distinctive call. Its ideal habitat for breeding is sea cliffs with crevices in which to nest and grassy cliff tops with plenty of insects to feed on. Keeping the habitat open by allowing grazing by ponies and cattle, and encouraging walkers to tramp the grass short, is helping to keep this little bird going. They bred successfully in 2002 and 2003, and a second nest was established in 2006, so it is hoped that numbers will continue to build up.

Photo: Toby Sawday

Along the southern coast of Devon, between Wembury and the river Exe, you may see another rare bird. A relative of the yellowhammer, the cirl bunting feeds on insects and seeds found in winter stubble and the weeds of arable field margins. Careful land management has allowed their numbers to flourish, from 118 pairs in 1989 to nearly 700 pairs in 2006.

Flowers love the coastal path, and bloom from early spring to autumn. Scurvy grass gives way to violets and primroses, then bluebells and local patches of spring squill. By May and June the cliffs are pink with thrift, white with sea campion and yellow with birdsfoot trefoil. Later, plants such as restharrow, wild carrot and hawkweeds will take their place. In south and east Devon wild orchids, early gentian and wild cabbage can be found.

In west Cornwall and east Devon coastal heath adds to the colour spectrum with swathes of purple heather and yellow gorse. Wooded sections – the most extensive of which are in north Devon – provide welcome shade in the summer, and a break from the open views to sea. The north coast oak woodlands grow on land that was difficult to cultivate, and some of the

Photos: Christopher Banks

trees are over 400 years old, providing habitat for a large number of plants and wildlife.

Sand dune systems at Rock, Penhale and Hayle in Cornwall, and at Braunton Burrows in North Devon, provide the perfect dry and salty conditions for sea holly and spurge, orchids, evening primrose and viper's bugloss.

Coastal path walkers will also be able to brush up on their geology as they stride, or stagger, along. About 370 million years ago the area that is now Devon and Cornwall was submerged in sea water which contained submarine volcanoes, sometimes active. The most dramatic results of these eruptions can be seen at Pentire Head, east of the Camel estuary.

Ever asked yourself how old the stones you're walking on are? South of a fault line between Polurrian Cove and Porthallow it is thought the rocks were formed deep in the earth's crust and were pushed up some 375 million years ago to form the Lizard Complex. Here there are fabulous examples of rich serpentine, smaller examples of which can be polished as souvenirs.

Turn away from the coast and look inland for a very different type of landscape – just as rewarding for walkers. Dartmoor (about 365 square miles) is the largest bit of wilderness you'll find in southern England, a beautiful stretch of grassy, heather-clad moor with granite eruptions that gives the walker a wonderful feeling of space. Apart from a few groups of chomping ponies and the odd sheep you won't meet a soul and you can do as much or as little as you like. It's the sort of place that people come to for a picnic in their car, just to look out on the magnificence of it all. There are

short walks along criss-crossed trails – generally speaking the southern parts are gentler and less demanding than the northern routes – and many of these are marked on signposts or with painted stones. Longer walks include parts of the Tarka Trail, Templar Way and the Two Moors Way.

Exmoor is a high plateau broken up by little woods and rivers – smaller than Dartmoor but, in parts, every bit as wild, and, because it's so close to the sea, it can suddenly be engulfed in mist and rain; make sure you take a waterproof. Walks are along a network of public paths, and there are guided walks for all abilities. In spite of its much smaller size, and the fact that a main road crosses it, Bodmin Moor has a particularly forbidding feel, but the walking is excellent, and archaeologists will be thrilled with the many relics of its Bronze Age population. Paths lead from all car parks, but watch out for the Beast!

There are public footpaths throughout the whole of Devon and Cornwall, criss-crossing both counties, joining up and leading away from major walks, taking you through farmland, forests, over rivers and through marshes. Many of the footpaths have handy parallel public transport routes, which means lazybones don't have to do an entire walk in one session. You can walk shorter distances to a pick-up point, or lengthen your walk by using public transport to link paths, so you can form a circuit.

Whether you choose the coastline or prefer to be inland, walking is the most intimate way of coming to know this very special part of England.

Nicola Crosse

Photo: Toby Sawday

Most people will tell you they like to go to the pub now and then. But which pub? Unless it's your local you won't know what to expect, and we all know that the dreary, the drab, do still exist. The pubs that have a miserable-looking display of limp petunias in a plastic pot outside, that reek of old beer and cooking oil, the ones with damp carpets, sticky tables, nicotine-brown walls – they pulse with thwarted ambition, slump in failure. They don't hum, there's just a clutch of rheumy-eyed old timers at the bar and a sour-faced couple in one corner – all of whom stare when you come in. They don't do food, just cheap crisps. To visit these pubs is a bit like visiting a zoo. The poor locals stare at you from their fixed positions as if they need rescuing.

So what makes a good pub? A good pub is merry, convivial. Somewhere to have a natter with friends, to relax and enjoy a drink and, if you are hungry, eat some good food. It doesn't even need to be complicated food – as long as the ingredients are as fresh and local as possible and they haven't been within a whisker of a microwave oven, you can't really go wrong.

In the main pages of this book you should be able to find a pub to suit you in either county. These places have rooms too, so you can make a night of it without worrying how you will get home. Some are simple, rustic; others will be more sophisticated than you expect. Wherever you decide to stay do know that pubs can be noisy places quite late into the night, so join in, or stay somewhere else!

Photo: www.dreamstime.com

Below are some more suggestions for pubs to visit by the coast and on rugged moors, timeless gems, community pubs, and pubs where food and drink are taken just as seriously as in the best restaurants.

By the sea

There's nothing better than having a sun-downer near the sea. Something about the air, the breeze, that feeling of having inhaled so much ozone, just lends itself to sitting in a good pub and putting the world to rights.

The Rashleigh Polkerris PL24 2TL (01726 813991). A pub on the beach, in a tiny cove!

The Shipwright's Arms Helford TR12 6JX (01326 231235). Pretty and thatched, with picnic benches at the water's edge.

The Pandora Inn Mylor Bridge TR11 5ST (01326 372678). Pontoon seating beside the pretty creek.

The Ship Inn Noss Mayo PL8 1EW (01752 872387). At the head of a tidal inlet with watery views.

The Ferry Boat Inn Dittisham TQ6 0EX (01803 722368). The only inn right on the river Dart, you can still arrive by boat.

Pilchard Inn Burgh Island TQ7 4BG (01548 810514). Walk across the sand to this atmospheric smuggler's pub on the tidal island.

On the moors

A hearty walk across any of the rugged moors in these counties will almost invariably bring on the desire for much refreshment.

Rugglestone Inn Widecombe-in-the-Moor TQ13 7TF (01364 621327). Tiny, rustic, and full of head-ducking beams.

Photos: The Bridge Inn

The Rock Inn Haytor Vale TQ13 9XP (01364 661305). Run by the same family for over 20 years, this civilised place oozes character.

The London Inn Molland EX36 3NG (01769 550269). Honest and unpretentious village local in the Exmoor foothills.

The Warren House Inn Postbridge PL20 6TA (01822 880208). Old tin miners' pub, high and alone, in a remote part of Dartmoor.

Timeless gems

These are often family-owned and little changed over the years, and a diminishing breed. At some you can expect few frills, just basic parlour rooms, lively banter, ale tapped from the cask and, if you're lucky, soup and sandwiches. Others may offer more in the way of food but remain genuinely unspoilt, classic examples of the great British pub.

The Star Inn St Just TR19 7LL (01736 788767). Proudly shirks the trappings of tourism and remains a drinkers' den. Community singing and joke-telling on Mondays.

The Bush Inn Morwenstow EX23 9SR (01288 331242). A genuinely ancient pub with seating on the front lawn and a view out to sea.

The Bridge Inn Topsham EX3 0QQ (01392 873862). One of England's last traditional ale houses, unchanged for most of the last century.

Community pubs

A well-loved pub with a big welcome, a crackling fire and the landlord's personality etched into the very fabric of the building lifts the spirits. Add heart-warming food and fine beer and you are in heaven. To have such a pub in your village would draw any community together and certainly beats meeting in a cold, soulless village hall.

Cadgwith Cove Inn Ruan Minor TR12 7JX (01326 290513). Smack on the Cornish coastal path, in a thatched fishing hamlet with views across the tiny working cove.

Duke of York Iddesleigh EX19 8BG (01837 810253). The most genuine of locals: a big-hearted, generous place with hearty home cooking.

Pig's Nose Inn East Prawle TQ7 2BY (01548 511209). Filled with character, cosy corners and quirky ephemera, it has an atmosphere all of its own.

Great food and drink

The horrid word 'gastropub' was born in London and rapidly embraced by the rest of the country. Whatever you want to call them, there's no denying that the average backstreet boozer has gone a lot posher – some completely over the top. But many have been transformed into thriving places where really good food is served and someone has put thought into the furniture and colours. These places serve local ales and freshly prepared food, sometimes simply but often imaginatively and with style.

Cornwall and Devon have been at the forefront of a return to 'real' food, partly because there's no shortage of locally bred, grown, caught or harvested produce, and partly because of a countrywide concern to reduce food miles and enjoy better tasting food.

Here we have Exmoor lamb, Devon Ruby Red beef, the freshest fish and shellfish from the coast, gorgeous butter, clotted cream and hand-made

Photo: Duke of York

cheeses. There's also 'scrumpy', English wines and a growing number of craft breweries producing ales that compete handsomely with the big boys.

The Gurnard's Head Zennor TR26 3DE (01736 796928). Super food, all homemade, wines generously priced, local ales on tap and log fires at both ends of the bar.

The Plume of Feathers Mitchell TR8 5AX (01872 510387). Delightful staff serve imaginative food and Sharp's Doom Bar is on tap.

Culm Valley Inn Culmstock EX15 3JJ (01884 840354). It may not be posh but it zings with great food, French wines from specialist growers and local beers tapped from the cask.

The Masons Arms Inn Knowstone EX36 4RY (01398 341231). Classic French and British dishes concocted from the finest regional produce, Cotleigh Tawny ale, fine French wines.

The Drewe Arms Broadhembury EX14 3NF (01404 841267). Otter ales tapped straight from the cask, wines beyond reproach and food that is way above average for a country pub.

The Jack in the Green Rockbeare EX5 2EE (01404 822240). Modern and mouthwatering variations of tried and trusted favourites at the bar; more ambitious delights in the restaurant.

The Dartmoor Inn Lydford EX20 4AY (01822 820221). Gourmet evenings, a Parisian bistro supper or a Brazilian jazz night: menus match the occasion and are all seasonal.

The Harris Arms Lewdown EX20 4PZ (01566 783331). They are members of the Slow Food movement so food is the

Photo: www.paulgroomphotography.com

west country's finest and wines are chosen from small growers.

The White Hart Bar Dartington TQ9 6EL (01803 847111). Organic and local produce are the mainstay of the menus, beers are from Otter Brewery, there are good wines, juices and ciders.

Kings Arms Strete TQ6 0RW (01803 770377). A naturally warm place with a fine menu, much of it fishy, and wide-ranging wines with an excellent number sold by the glass.

Rose & Crown Yealmpton PL8 2EB (01752 880223). Staff are cheerful, the best wines represent the best value, and the ales and the menu change monthly.

Nicola Crosse & David Hancock

You needn't be stuck for ideas when the weather is less than perfect and you have children to entertain – Devon and Cornwall have much to inspire children of all ages.

Look and learn

At the National Maritime Museum Cornwall, Falmouth (01326 313388; www.nmmc.co.uk) there's all sorts to keep the whole family busy including exhibitions and displays, workshops (for example knots and rope making, or designing a surfboard and wetsuit) as well as the ever-popular Museum Minnows for under fives.

The National Marine Aquarium, Plymouth (01752 600301; www.national-aquarium.co.uk) is well worth a visit – don't miss the walk-through tunnel, where sharks cruise above your head.

Be dazzled by more than 1,000,000 plants representing 5,000 species from many of the climatic zones of the world at the Eden Project, St Austell (01726 811911; www.edenproject.com). There are two huge biomes – the biggest conservatories in the world – which are great for children who love to see, touch and smell the plants that chocolate, chewing gum and bananas come from.

Photos: www.istockphotos.com

Young children are usually interested in history, so why not head off to Geevor Tin Mine, Pendeen (01736 788662; www.geevor.com) the largest preserved mining site in the UK and a working mine until 1990. It is now a museum and heritage centre, where you can learn about Cornwall's mining history, with many surface buildings, a guided underground tour, mineral gallery, a shop and a café.

For fascinating, free fun go to House of Marbles, Bovey Tracey (01626 835285; www.houseofmarbles.com) – a museum of marbles, glass games and Bovey Tracey pottery. You'll find the Monster Marble Run, an antique marble-making machine, a large collection of toys and games, glass blowing and wonderful exhibitions of glass and china. There are a shop and restaurant too so you can spend a few happy hours there on a gloomy day.

Arts and crafts

If you've got creative youngsters, try out The Cardew Teapottery, Bovey Tracey (01626 832172; www.craftsatcardew.co.uk), where adults and children can make and decorate their own pots. Entry is free and there's the Madhatter's Restaurant and a ten-acre woodland playground too.

St Ives is full of things to do on a wet day – there are wonderful shops, galleries, cafes, restaurants, bars, and of course Tate St Ives (01736 796226; www.tate.org.uk/stives) which puts on four exhibitions a year, plus displays and events.

Wildlife and nature

If your kids are interested in wildlife, the choice is wonderfully varied.

Have they always wanted to know about the shy and mysterious badger? Go to Devon Badger Watch near Tiverton for an amazing evening (01398 351506; www.devonbadgerwatch.co.uk).

For an informative family visit, try Dartmoor Otters and Buckfast Butterflies, Buckfastleigh (01364 642916; www.ottersandbutterflies.co.uk). See how new butterflies emerge in tropical surroundings and watch the otters swimming underwater.

There is masses to do at the Prickly Ball Farm and Hedgehog Hospital, East Ogwell (01626 362319): learn about hedgehogs, feed lambs, walk a goat or ferret, groom a pony and cuddle any number of furry pets. By visiting the farm you are helping to support the hospital – about 200 hedgehogs a year are rescued, with the aim of releasing them back into the wild when fully recovered. There's Hoglet's coffee shop too when you need a rest and a snack.

Even when it's rainy Paignton Zoo (01803 697500; www.paigntonzoo.org.uk) is a great day out for everyone. As well as the thousands of animals and plants, there's a miniature train ride, a wobbly jungle bridge in Lemur Wood, indoor and outdoor play areas, keeper talks and feeding times, places to eat and places to sit – all packed into eighty acres of natural habitat.

At Roskilly's of Cornwall, Tregellast Barton (01326 280479; www.roskillys.co.uk) watch the cows being milked and see ice cream and fudge-making demonstrations at this organic farm. There are crafts, walks, ponds and tearooms with homemade food.

Boat trips

Boat trips can still be fun on damp days, if you have waterproof clothing!

Take a boat trip on the Fal Estuary, the third largest natural harbour in the world; boats leave from Prince of Wales Pier, Custom House Quay and St Mawes Harbour. Cross to Falmouth or cruise up the creek to Truro.

Trips up the River Dart can be taken from Totnes, a bustling town with many

Photos: istock.com

independent shops and good places to eat. It's fun to hop on a steam train from Buckfastleigh (South Devon Railway, 0845 345 1420), chug to Totnes then catch a boat which takes you down the Dart to Dartmouth.

The Red Pig passenger ferry from Cawsand into the heart of Plymouth is a great thirty-minute boat trip, giving you the best views of the city without a car. Boats leave Ilfracombe three times a week for Lundy Island, a small island owned by the National Trust and managed by the Landmark Trust, and a haven for birds, wild ponies and seals.

Outdoor action

If your family just love to be outside whatever the weather, try kayaking, climbing, body boarding, canoeing, caving and more, at Mountain Water Experience, Kingsbridge (01548 550675; www.mountainwater experience.co.uk).

In Newquay, O'Neill Surf Academy (01637 876083; www.oneillsurf academy.co.uk) has a Kids' Surf Club, where eight- to twelve-year-olds can learn to surf safely, have fun and meet other kids.

You can, of course, just brave the beach in the rain and get wet – set up a beach tent, take a wetsuit and flasks of hot drinks and go swimming or surfing on this stunning coast.

Cycling

How about cycling in the rain? Dress up warm with hats and waterproofs and head out to Wadebridge, where Bridge Bike Hire (01208 813050; www.bridgebikehire.co.uk) rents out a wonderfully eccentric range of bikes to suit everyone.

Or you can follow the Tarka Trail, a 180-mile looping route through north and mid Devon. The trail between Barnstaple and Torrington takes the route of a disused railway line and is particularly suited for both cyclists and walkers.

Eating

After all that exercise you'll be peckish, and luckily Devon and Cornwall have fantastic places to eat out. Escape from the rain in Pig Finca Café, Kingsbridge

(01548 855777; www.pigfinca.co.uk) – an alternative, relaxed venue for food, art and music.

Treat the kids to some fish and chips from The Cod Father in Kingsbridge, or go to The Gurnard's Head, near Zennor, and have some cooked by the great chef there. And try Annie's famous pasties in Lizard village.

For a special organic shopping trip and delicious lunch, visit the Field Kitchen at Riverford Farm Shop in Buckfastleigh (01803 762074; www.riverfordfarmshop.co.uk). You need to book beforehand to go on one of the tours or trips at the farm and then have lunch – informal and hands-on with tractor and trailer rides and lots of touching, smelling and tasting.

Go to the popular Alf Resco, Dartmouth (01803 835880; www.cafealfresco.co.uk) both for the atmosphere and the setting.

Start Bay Inn, Torcross (01548 580 553) is an easygoing family inn with a great selection of food, including fresh-as-a-daisy fish (some caught by the landlord).

The Oyster Shack, Bigbury (01548 810876; www.oystershack.co.uk) is the place to experience fresh, local seafood, cooked simply.

The Avocet Café, Topsham (01392 877887) is a bustling little place, serving good food at lunchtime and homebaked cakes and pastries during the day.

Wendy Ogden

Not being the 'outdoorsy' type, I was surprised to find myself, last September, booking in for a day of watery fun near Fowey. Given that my previous experiences of outdoor pursuits had seen me running over a dog with a canoe on the Wye and dangling upside down off a seventy-foot cliff in an abseiling 'mishap', I was not the most obvious of candidates. But I was keen to have another go so, with an old university friend in tow, I set off for Cornwall.

Shortly after turning off the A30, and negotiating several meandering country lanes, we found ourselves pulling into a well-organised yard. Two Canadian canoes sat on a trailer in a corner, but before we had time to imagine ourselves in them we were enthusiastically greeted by Ella, a twenty-month-old labrador pup. David, her owner (and our instructor for the day), followed closely behind.

Photos: David Collin

Over a pre-adventure coffee in David's fabulous farmhouse kitchen we were shown a map of the journey we would be taking up the Fowey river – and to our relief, were told we would not be doing the ten-kilometre trip. David, I am glad to report, is keen to tailor your adventure to what you are comfortable with. He was also – at my request – happy to show us around his two self-catering cottages and his yurt. With its wooden floor and a wood-fired hot tub right outside, this constitutes classy camping! Verity and I were busy planning a thrilling girls' weekend away when the sight of the canoes brought us back to earth.

David loaned us each a waterproof bag for our spare clothing and picnic lunch, then we jumped in to the minibus and headed down to the river. Memories of my days as a girl guide came flooding back as David attempted to teach us a variety of knots to secure the bags to our canoe. Patiently he showed us again and again while we fumbled with loops and rope ends, with moderate success.

Verity and I were in one canoe, David and the dog in the other. I was to sit at the back and do the steering, so once I'd jumped in David talked me through the moves: 'J' strokes to turn left, 'C' strokes to turn right. Natural logic and spatial awareness are not skills I am blessed with but I did begin to get the hang of it.

Verity followed me in and with a push we were off. Squealing with excitement we headed straight for a little boat docked in the small harbour. I immediately put my 'J' stroke into action – and it worked. I have no idea what I was expecting but I was impressed all the same. Then, to ensure we were paddling together, David asked us to turn the canoe in a full circle. When I paddled forwards on my left, Verity paddled backwards on her right. And so we learnt to reverse, to paddle in a straight line and, most useful of all, to stop.

We headed away from Fowey upriver, and found ourselves surrounded by trees on all sides. As we glided along David chatted knowledgably about the area, the buildings and the birdlife. The sun poked out from the clouds, a breeze picked up and we broke into smiles. It was Ella's maiden voyage and within minutes she had leapt out of David's canoe and was swimming alongside us.

Apart from the tinkling of the buoys and the splashing of the cormorants – one minute under the surface, the next reappearing some distance away – there was hardly a sound. A rare moment of peace.

After forty minutes of hard paddling we approached a village and decided to pull over for a cider break. It was a wonderful experience, paddling up to the shore, dragging the canoes onto the sand, taking a quick, cold drink in the pub by the water, then jumping back in and paddling off again. So much more liberating than travelling by car.

We stopped again for a picnic lunch on an empty stretch of shore, and to our delight David made us a mug of tea from a Kelly kettle, traditionally used by Irish fishermen. Sitting on the edge of the water in the hazy sunshine, wood crackling beneath the kettle, Ella snuggling up beside us, I mused out loud that this, surely, was how life was meant to be. David, as it happens, is an enthusiastic advocate of the 'slow' movement, cares for the environment and aims to be carbon-neutral within the next couple of years; two windmills are planned on his land to help with this.

I could have lounged on that river bank for days (maybe next time I'll sign up for an overnight expedition), but it was high tide and time for us to head back. Our arms already weary, we prepared ourselves to paddle against both tide and wind.

For the homeward journey we were joined by Ella, who alternated between standing at the prow – our own figurehead – and leaning over the edge, paws dangling in the water. There was a moment of panic when we drifted a little too close to the edge, into the trees and weeds, but our new-found paddling and steering skills soon got us

Photos: David Collin

out of trouble. We were barely able to conceal our smiles.

Sooner than we realised, but almost five hours after we had left, we were back at the starting point. We had just enough energy left to help David pull the canoes onto the trailer before sinking into the minibus. A night in the cosy yurt would have been very nice but we had to face the M5 instead. However, the memories of our little adventure, of the beautiful surroundings, the fresh air and the magnificent peace, saw us through. Perhaps I am an 'outdoorsy' type after all?

Rebecca Thomas

Rebecca enjoyed a day out with Adventure Cornwall (www. adventurecornwall.co.uk). *See also entry 163.*

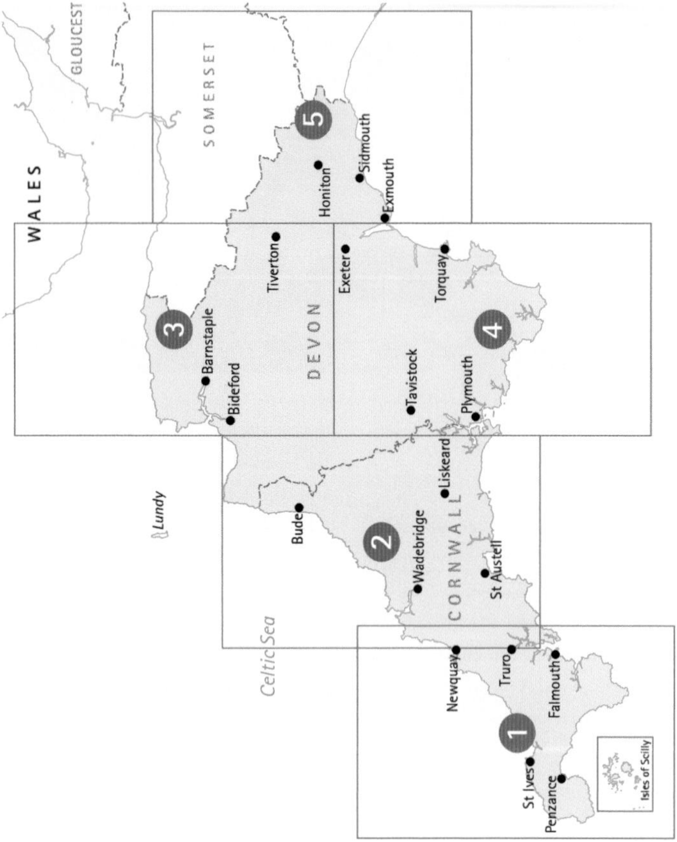
WALES
GLOUCEST
SOMERSET
DEVON
CORNWALL
Lundy
Celtic Sea
Isles of Scilly
1
2
3
4
5
Honiton
Sidmouth
Exmouth
Tiverton
Exeter
Torquay
Barnstaple
Bideford
Tavistock
Plymouth
Liskeard
Bude
Wadebridge
St Austell
Newquay
Truro
Falmouth
St Ives
Penzance

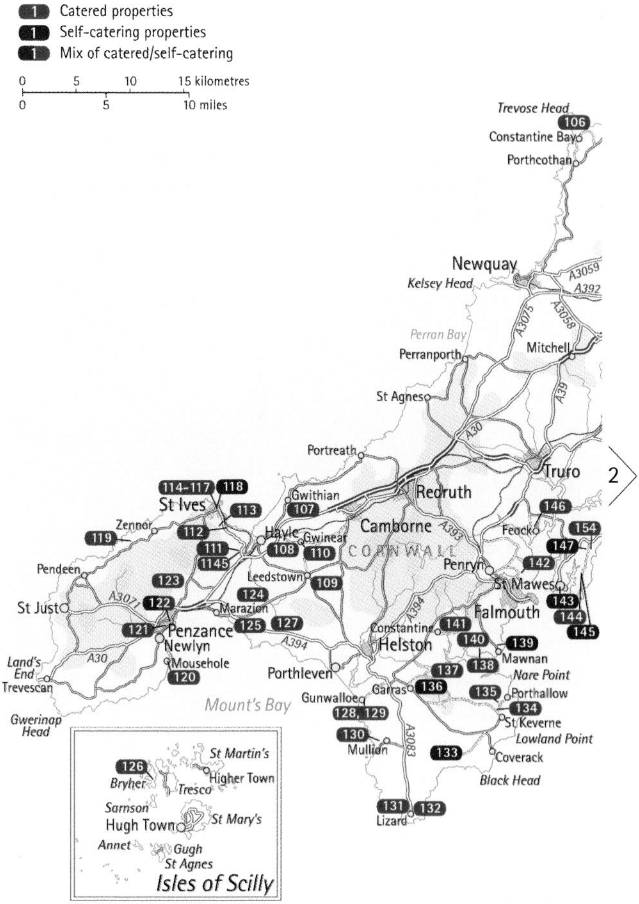

45

Legend:
- 1 Catered properties
- 1 Self-catering properties
- 1 Mix of catered/self-catering

0 5 10 15 kilometres
0 5 10 miles

Trevose Head — 106
Constantine Bay
Porthcothan

Newquay
Kelsey Head
A3059
A392

Perran Bay
Perranporth
Mitchell

St Agnes

Portreath
Truro — 2

114–117 118
St Ives
113
Gwithian
Redruth
146

119 Zennor
112
Hayle Gwinear
Camborne
154
147

111
108 110
CORNWALL
Penryn
St Mawes
142
143

123
1145
Leedstown
109
Feock

St Just
A3071
122
124
Marazion
Falmouth
141
140
139
145

121
125 127
A394
Constantine
Helston
Mawnan
Nare Point

Penzance
Newlyn
137 138
135 Porthallow

Mousehole
120
Porthleven
Gunwalloe
136
134 St Keverne

Pendeen
Land's End
Trevescan
A30
Lowland Point

Gwerinap Head
Mount's Bay
128, 129
130
Mullion
133
Coverack
Black Head

126 St Martin's
Bryher Higher Town
Tresco
Samson
St Mary's
Hugh Town St Agnes
Annet Gugh St Agnes
131 132
Lizard

Isles of Scilly

©Maidenhead Cartographic, 2008

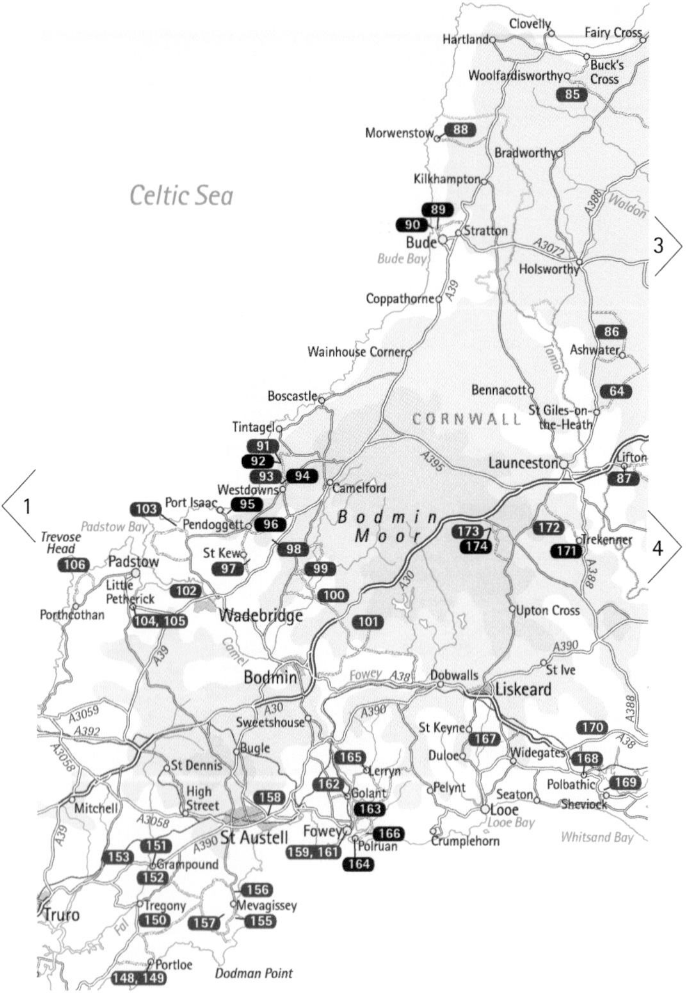
Clovelly
Hartland
Fairy Cross
Buck's Cross
Woolfardisworthy
85
Morwenstow
88
Bradworthy
Kilkhampton
Celtic Sea
89
90
Stratton
Bude
Bude Bay
A3072
Holsworthy
3
Coppathorne
A39
86
Ashwater
Wainhouse Corner
Tamar
Bennacott
64
Boscastle
St Giles-on-the-Heath
CORNWALL
Tintagel
91
92
A395
Launceston
Lifton
93
94
87
Westdowns
Camelford
1
103
Port Isaac
95
Padstow Bay
Pendoggett
96
Bodmin Moor
173
174
172
Trekenner
171
4
Trevose Head
106
Padstow
St Kew
97
98
99
A388
Little Petherick
102
100
A30
Porthcothan
104, 105
Wadebridge
101
Upton Cross
A39
Camel
A390
St Ive
Bodmin
Fowey
A38
Dobwalls
Liskeard
A3059
A30
A392
Sweetshouse
A390
St Keyne
170
167
A3058
Bugle
Duloe
Widegates
168
St Dennis
165
Lerryn
162
Pelynt
Polbathic
169
High Street
158
Golant
Seaton
Sheviock
Mitchell
163
Looe
Looe Bay
A3058
Fowey
166
Whitsand Bay
A390
St Austell
Polruan
Crumplehorn
A39
151
153
159, 161
164
Grampound
152
156
Tregony
Mevagissey
Truro
150
157
155
Fal
Portloe
Dodman Point
148, 149

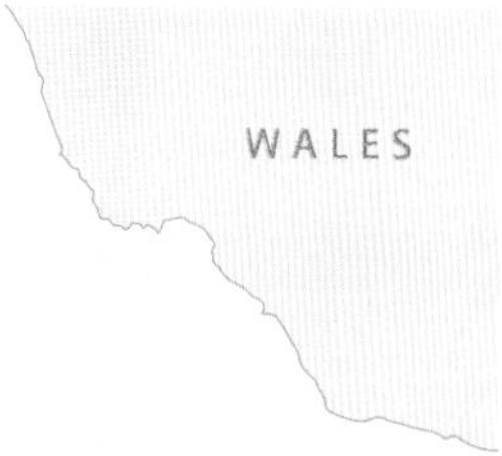

47

WALES

SOMERSET

DEVON

Exmoor National Park

72 Lynton
71 Foreland Point
73 Martinhoe
74 Ilfracombe
Lee
75 Mortehoe
Woolacombe
Saunton
Braunton
Bittadon 78
76 Kentisbury
77
79
Bratton Fleming
70 Heasley Mill
69 Upcott
Barnstaple
Norham
Bideford
Newton Tracey
Atherington
South Molton
84 Landcross
2 Buckland Brewer
Great Torrington
80 Chittlehamholt
82 King's Nympton 81
Alswear
68 Bampton
67
Stibb Cross
Merton
Dolton
83 Hollocombe
Chulmleigh
Witheridge
Templeton
66 Loxbeare
5
Tiverton
Winkleigh
65 Cheriton Fitzpaine
Hatherleigh
Highampton
Copplestone
Halwill Junction
Crediton
Broadclyst
4
©Maidenhead Cartographic, 2008

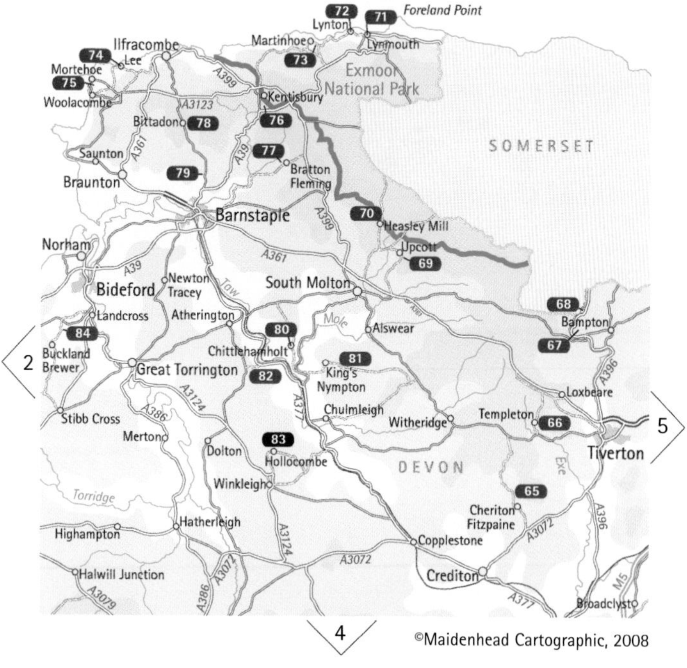

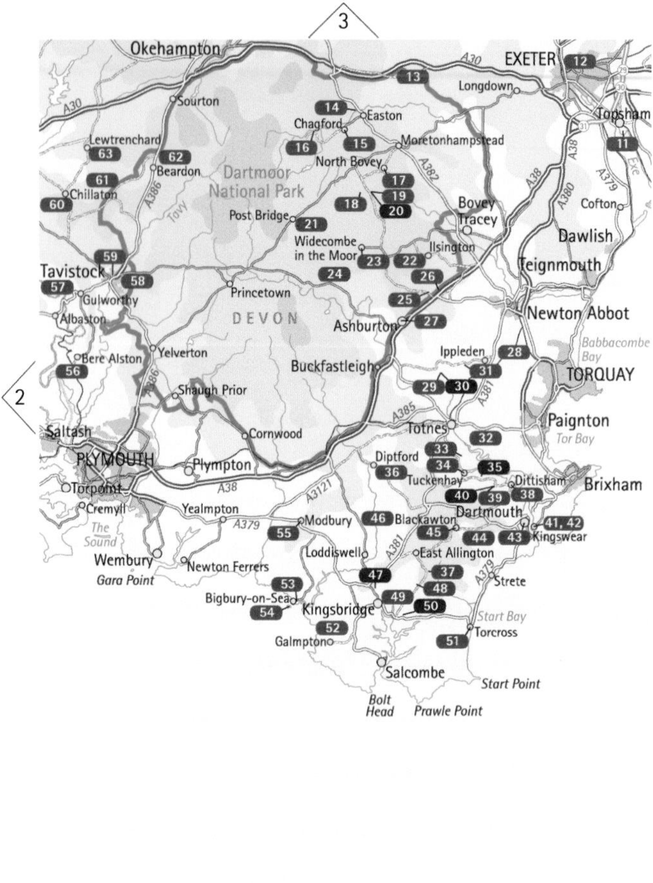
3
2
Okehampton
EXETER
Longdown
Sourton
Easton
Chagford
Topsham
Moretonhampstead
Lewtrenchard
Beardon
Dartmoor
National Park
North Bovey
Chillaton
Cofton
Bovey
Tracey
Post Bridge
Dawlish
Widecombe
in the Moor
Ilsington
Teignmouth
Tavistock
Princetown
Gulworthy
Albaston
DEVON
Newton Abbot
Ashburton
Babbacombe
Bay
Ippleden
Bere Alston
Yelverton
TORQUAY
Buckfastleigh
Shaugh Prior
Paignton
Tor Bay
Saltash
Totnes
Cornwood
PLYMOUTH
Plympton
Diptford
Torpoint
Tuckenhay
Dittisham
Brixham
Cremyll
Yealmpton
Dartmouth
Modbury
Blackawton
The
Sound
Kingswear
Loddiswell
East Allington
Wembury
Newton Ferrers
Gara Point
Strete
Bigbury-on-Sea
Kingsbridge
Start Bay
Torcross
Galmpton
Salcombe
Start Point
Bolt
Head
Prawle Point
A30
A38
A386
A382
A380
A379
A385
A381
A3121
Tavy
Exe
1
2
3
4
5
6
7
8
9
10
11
12
13
14
15
16
17
18
19
20
21
22
23
24
25
26
27
28
29
30
31
32
33
34
35
36
37
38
39
40
41, 42
43
44
45
46
47
48
49
50
51
52
53
54
55
56
57
58
59
60
61
62
63

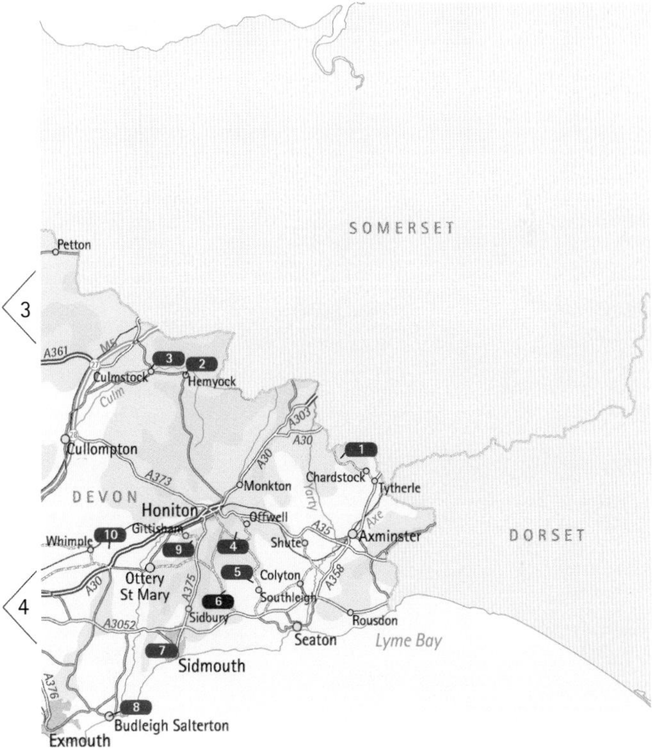
SOMERSET
Petton
3
A361
Culmstock
Hemyock
Culm
Cullompton
A373
DEVON
Honiton
Monkton
A30
A303
Chardstock
Tytherle
Yarty
Offwell
A35
Axminster
Axe
DORSET
Whimple
Gittisham
10
9
4
Shute
5
Colyton
Ottery
St Mary
A375
A358
4
6
Southleigh
Sidbury
A3052
Rousdon
Seaton
Lyme Bay
7
Sidmouth
A376
8
Budleigh Salterton
Exmouth
1
2

Devon

Photo: Christopher Banks

Applebarn Cottage

A tree-lined drive leads to a long white wall; a gate in the wall opens to an explosion of colour – the garden. Come for a deliciously restful place and the nicest hosts. The wisteria-covered 17th-century cottage is full of books, flowers and paintings, and bedrooms are large, traditional and wonderfully comfortable, with all-white bathrooms. One of the rooms is in an extension but blends in beautifully. Breakfast, served in a lovely slate-floored dining room, includes a neighbour's homemade honey. Eat in if you can: dinner is superb and includes vegetables and fruits from the garden.

Price	Half-board £56-£60 p.p.
Rooms	2 suites.
Meals	Dinner included. Pub/restaurant 3 miles.
Closed	Last two weeks November up to 1 March.
Directions	A30 from Chard, signed Honiton. Left at top of hill signed Wambrook/Stockland. After 3 miles pass Ferne Animal Sanctuary. Straight on at next x-roads (Membury); 0.75 miles, left, signed Cotley/Ridge. Past Hartshill Boarding Kennels; signed 2nd right.

Patricia & Robert Spencer
Bewley Down, Membury, Axminster EX13 7JX
Tel 01460 220873
Web www.applebarn-cottage.co.uk

Regency House

Rooms are beautifully proportioned in this 1855 rectory, with varnished floors and rugs downstairs. Both the music room and the drawing room have floor-to-ceiling windows overlooking the lake and the glorious garden that Jenny has created. She also adores collecting pictures and there are some interesting contemporary paintings and hunting prints around and lots of books too. The large, comfortable and light bedroom is decorated in classic pale creamy colours and still has the original shutters. You have breakfast in the dining area of the huge farmhouse kitchen warmed by the Aga.

Price	£90. Singles £45.
Rooms	1 double.
Meals	Dinner £25. Pub 3 miles.
Closed	Rarely.
Directions	M5 junc. 26 for Wellington, from north. Left at roundabout; immed. right at junction, left at next junction. Right at top of hill. Left at x-roads. In Hemyock take Dunkeswell/Honiton Road. House 500 yds on right.

Mrs Jenny Parsons
Hemyock, Cullompton EX15 3RQ

Tel 01823 680238
Email jenny.parsons@btinternet.com

Culm Valley Inn

This may not be posh but it's warm, easy and charming: deep pink-washed walls, glowing coals, flickering candles. From ragged bar stools sample microbrewery beers and unusually good food. Look to the chalkboard for south coast seafood, weekend fish specials (monkfish with crispy ginger and garlic noodles), Ruby Red Devon beef from nearby farms, and tapas. Thirsty? Order from a fantastic array of rare and curious spirits, French wines from specialist growers and local beers tapped from the cask. Bedrooms are simple and cheerful, with white bed linen and vibrant walls, and share two spotless bathrooms.

Price	From £55. Singles £30.
Rooms	3: 1 double, 1 twin, 1 family from £55. Singles £30.
Meals	Main courses £7-£20; bar meals £6-£10.
Closed	3pm-7pm. Open all day weekends and in summer.
Directions	On B3391, 2 miles off A38 west of Wellington.

Richard Hartley
Culmstock, Cullompton EX15 3JJ

Tel	01884 840354
Email	culmvalleyinn@btinternet.com

West Colwell Farm

Devon lanes, pheasants, bluebell walks *and* sparkling B&B. The Hayes clearly love what they do; ex-TV producers, they have converted this 18th-century farmhouse and barns into a cosy, warm and stylish place to stay. Be charmed by original beams and pine doors, heritage colours and clean lines. Bedrooms feel self-contained, two have terraces overlooking the wooded valley and the largest is tucked under the roof. Linen is luxurious, showers are huge and breakfasts (Frank's pancakes, lovely bacon, eggs from next door) are totally flexible. A pretty garden in front, beaches nearby, peace all around. Bliss.

Price	From £70. Singles £50.
Rooms	3 doubles.
Meals	Restaurants in Honiton.
Closed	Christmas.
Directions	3 miles from Honiton; Offwell signed off A35 Honiton-Axminster road. In centre of village, at church, down hill. Farm 0.5 miles on.

Frank & Carol Hayes
Offwell, Honiton EX14 9SL

Tel 01404 831130
Web www.westcolwell.co.uk

Glebe House

Set on a hillside with fabulous views over the Coly valley, this late-Georgian vicarage has become a heart-warming B&B. The views will entice you, the hosts will delight you and the house is filled with interesting things. Chuck and Emma spent many years at sea – he a Master Mariner, she a chef – and have filled these big light rooms with cushions, kilims and treasured family pieces. There's a sitting room for guests, a sweet conservatory with a vintage vine, peaceful bedrooms with blissful views and bathrooms that sparkle. All this, three goats, wildlife beyond the ha-ha and the fabulous coast a hike away.

Price	From £60. Singles £40.
Rooms	3: 1 double, 1 twin/double, 1 family room.
Meals	Pubs/restaurants 2.5 miles.
Closed	Christmas & New Year.
Directions	A375 from Honiton; left opposite Hare & Hounds on B3174 to Seaton. 2nd left to Southleigh, 1.5 miles. In village 1st left to Northleigh; 600 yds, drive on left.

Emma & Chuck Guest
Southleigh, Colyton EX24 6SD

Tel 01404 871276
Web www.guestsatglebe.com

Higher Wiscombe

The Old Winery is perfect for family reunions: 20 can easily be accommodated in the 10 bedrooms, there are two kitchens, a sitting room with a wood-burner, a dining room with an oak table that seats 32. The barns are smaller; both have range cookers, squashy sofas, books, cosy wood-burners. Each has its own patio area and garden complete with barbecues and stunning views; the central courtyard and outdoor heated pool (separate time slots for separate parties) are shared. The attention to detail is superb (champagne buckets, Green Tourism awards), and beaches and coastal path are four miles away.

Price	Old Winery: £1,795–£4,250. Thatched Barn & Flint Barn: £475-£1,195. Prices per week.
Rooms	Old Winery for 20. Thatched Barn for 6. Flint Barn for 6.
Meals	Restaurant/pub within 20-minute walk.
Closed	Never.
Directions	Directions given on booking.

Lorna Handyside
Southleigh, Colyton EX24 6JF

Tel 01404 871360
Web www.higherwiscombe.com

Rose Cottage

Step back in time to seaside fun and bracing walks. Tucked down a quiet street in sleepy Sidmouth, this is a quick hop to the beach – why not rent the family's beach hut? – or onto the coastal path. With stripped pine floorboards, stained-glass features and pretty cushions, Jackie has created a friendly, homely place. Bedrooms are small but jolly with quilted covers and sunny walls, two have tiny showers, another has a slipper bath. There's homemade muesli and organic bacon for breakfast in a room with a seaside teashop feel; no sitting room but a large garden with a slide and swing for children.

Price	From £70. Singles from £55.
Rooms	4: 2 doubles, 1 twin; 1 double with separate bath.
Meals	Packed lunch £5. Pubs/restaurants 300 yds.
Closed	Christmas, New Year & occasionally.
Directions	From Exeter A3052 to Sidmouth. Over r'bout at Woodlands Hotel. House is 100 yards on left just before zebra crossing.

Jacalyn & Neil Cole
Coburg Road, Sidmouth EX10 8NF

Tel 01395 577179
Web www.rosecottage-sidmouth.co.uk

Simcoe House

A gem of a setting, this gracious 1790 house built for General John Simcoe is within strolling distance of the beach and town. There are stunning views from wide windows in the lovely guest sitting room, so find a book and settle in a comfy chair while the sun streams in. Jane gives you breakfast in the pretty conservatory or the dining room. Bedrooms are sunny and charming with fresh flowers and fabulous vistas. Laze on the terrace, look up the house history in the local museum or relish the Jurassic coast. A unique house with a beachy feel and delightful owners. *Children over ten welcome.*

Price	£70-£80. Singles £50.
Rooms	2: 1 double, 1 twin.
Meals	Pubs/restaurants 5-minute walk.
Closed	Christmas.
Directions	M5 junc. 30 onto A376. Then B3179 to Budleigh Salterton (approx. 8 miles). Into town centre then left opposite The Creamery, onto Fore Street Hill. 300 yds on right.

Jane Crosse
8 Fore Street Hill, Budleigh Salterton EX9 6PE
Tel 01395 446013
Email simcoehouse@hotmail.co.uk

Combe House Hotel & Restaurant

A sensational setting: 3,500 acres with a 'lost' arboretum and a long, meandering approach; this mullion-windowed Grade I manor is a very special place and the staff are delightful. Fabulous food, the best Devon produce, is served in the dining room or the Georgian kitchen by the glow of Tilley lamps and candles. Bedrooms are a good size with antiques and large beds, one has a huge round copper bath. Most atmospheric of all is the entrance hall with its carved fireplace – grab a book and settle here on one of the many comfy sofas. Or head for the coast; it's nearer than you might think. *Minimum stay two nights at weekends.*

Price	£164-£254. Singles from £134. Suites £308. Half-board from £115 p.p.
Rooms	15: 10 twins/doubles, 1 four-poster, 4 suites.
Meals	Lunch £20-£26. Dinner £39.50. Private parties in Georgian kitchen from £39.50 p.p. plus room hire.
Closed	Rarely.
Directions	M5 junc. 28 or 29 to Honiton, then Sidmouth. A375 south for a mile. House signed right through woods.

Ruth & Ken Hunt
Gittisham, Honiton, Exeter EX14 3AD

Tel 01404 540400
Web www.thishotel.com

Larkbeare Grange

Expectations rise as you follow the tree-lined drive to the immaculate Georgian house… and are met, the second you enter this elegant, calm and characterful home. The upkeep is perfect, the feel is chic and the whole place exudes well-being. Sparkling sash windows fill big rooms with light, floors shine and the old grandfather clock ticks away the hours. Expect the best: goose down duvets on king-size beds, contemporary luxury in fabric and fitting, flexible breakfasts and lovely long views from the bedroom at the front. Charlie, Savoy-trained, and Julia are charming and fun: you are in perfect hands. *Green Tourism Business Scheme Silver Leaf.*

Price	£88-£110. Singles from £73.
Rooms	3: 2 doubles, 1 twin/double.
Meals	Supper from £18.50. BYO. Pub 1.5 miles.
Closed	Rarely.
Directions	From A30 Exmouth & Ottery St Mary junc. At r'bouts follow Whimple signs. 0.25 miles, right; 0.5 miles, left signed Larkbeare. House 1 mile on left.

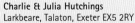

Charlie & Julia Hutchings
Larkbeare, Talaton, Exeter EX5 2RY

Tel 01404 822069
Web www.larkbeare.net

Beach House

Lapping at the riverside garden is the Exe estuary, wide and serene. Birds and boats, the soft hills beyond, a gorgeous Georgian house on the river and kind hosts who have been here for years. The garden is beautiful, full of topiary, old apple trees and box hedging; you may breakfast in the conservatory or in the dining room – enjoy raspberries and blackberries in season. No guest sitting room but comfy chairs in the bedrooms, which are soft and chintzy, with antique white bedspreads, charmingly old-fashioned bathrooms and estuary views. Cycle into Exeter, for culture and Cathedral.

Price	£80. Singles £45.
Rooms	2: 1 twin, 1 double.
Meals	Pubs/restaurants 8-minute walk.
Closed	Christmas & New Year; January-end March.
Directions	M5 exit 30; signs to Exmouth. Right at George & Dragon. After 1 mile, immed. left after level crossing. At mini r'bout, left down The Strand. House last on left by beach.

Trevor & Jane Coleman
The Strand, Topsham, Exeter EX3 0BB

Tel 01392 876456
Email janecoleman45@hotmail.com

The Garden House

Refulgent! An extraordinary restoration of a 1930s house, carried out with passion and joy. Bedrooms are sumptuous and filled with all you might need; beds plump with cushions, fabrics smooth, colours vibrant, scents divine. The exuberance reaches the garden; Jane's energy among the pots, quirky topiary and tulips is almost palpable. A huge collection of books are stacked hither and thither, the chandeliers sparkle, candles flicker and there's a vast choice of breakfasts, beautifully served. It may not be minimalist but it is deeply comfortable, good-humoured and an easy walk into the city.

Price	£75-£80. Singles £40.
Rooms	3: 1 double; 1 twin, 1 single sharing bath.
Meals	Pubs/restaurants nearby.
Closed	Rarely.
Directions	M5 junc. 30 for city centre & university. Behind Debenhams, Longbrook St into Pennsylvania Rd. Through lights, 2nd left into Hoopern Ave; house at end on left.

David & Jane Woolcock
4 Hoopern Avenue, Pennsylvania, Exeter EX4 6DN

Tel 01392 256255
Web www.exeterbedandbreakfast.co.uk

Higher Eggbeer Farm

Over 900 years old and still humming with life: pigs, cows, ponies, rabbits, and chickens share the rambling gardens. Sally Anne and William are artistic, fun, slightly wacky and eccentric. It's an adventure to stay, so keep an open mind: the house is a historic gem and undeniably rustic. Huge inglenook fireplaces, interesting art, books, piano, wellies, muddle and charm. Your lovely hosts will take children to feed animals and collect eggs, and will babysit. Be wrapped in peace in your own half of the house (with beautiful drawing room), immersed in a magnificent panorama of forest, hills and fields of waving wheat.

Price	£55-£70. Singles £40.
Rooms	3: 2 twins/doubles sharing bath (2nd room let to same party); 1 double in main house sharing bath.
Meals	Restaurants in village, 5-minute walk.
Closed	Rarely.
Directions	A30 to Okehampton. After 10 miles left to C. Bishop; 1st left after Old Thatch pub. Down & up hill; down private lane on right after sharp left.

Sally Anne & William Selwyn
Cheriton Bishop, Exeter EX6 6JQ
Tel 01647 24427

Sandy Park Inn

This is a cracking country boozer, loved by locals, with food that punches above its weight; Barry the butcher brings in slow-grown pork off the moor, the cod comes battered in beer, the cheeses are all local. It's snug, with low ceilings, flagged floors and huge knots of wood crackling in an old stone fire. Bedrooms sparkle with unexpected treats, all have pretty views over the village, some are en suite, some not. The bar is lively, sometimes with live music, so this will only suit those who want to join in with the fun. Also: kippers at breakfast, maps for walkers and dog biscuits behind the bar.

Price	£92. Singles £59.
Rooms	5: 1 twin, 1 double; 3 doubles each with separate bath or shower.
Meals	Lunch from £5. Dinner from £8.
Closed	Never.
Directions	A30 west from Exeter to Whiddon Cross. South 2 miles to Sandy Park. Pub on right at x-roads.

Nick Rout
Sandy Park, Chagford TQ13 8JW
Tel 01647 433267
Web www.sandyparkinn.co.uk

Cyprian's Cot

A charming terraced cottage of 16th-century nooks and crannies and beams worth ducking. The setting is exquisite: the garden leads into fields of sheep, the Dartmoor Way goes through the town and the Two Moors Way skirts it. Shelagh, a lovely lady, gives guests their own sitting room with a fire, lit on cool nights; breakfasts, served in the cosy dining room, are fresh, free-range and tasty. Up the narrow stairs and into simple bedrooms – a small double and a tiny twin. A perfect house and hostess, and a perfect little town to discover, with its pubs, fine restaurant and delicatessen, organic shop and tearoom.

Price	£55. Singles from £30.
Rooms	2: 1 twin; 1 double with separate bath.
Meals	Pubs/restaurants in village.
Closed	Rarely.
Directions	In Chagford pass church on left; 1st right beyond Globe Inn opposite. House 150 yds on right.

Shelagh Weeden
47 New Street, Chagford TQ13 8BB

Tel 01647 432256
Web www.cyprianscot.co.uk

Gidleigh Park

Gidleigh stands in 45 acres of lush silence with the North Teign river pottering through and huge views shooting off to Meldon Hill. Inside, you find a faultless country house. A fire smoulders in the oak-panelled hall, ferns tumble from silver champagne bowls, sofas come crisply dressed in dazzling fabrics. Bedrooms are divine, impeccably presented with hand-stitched linen, woollen blankets, upholstered headboards and polished wooden furniture. As for the food, Michael Caines brings two Michelin stars to the table, so expect the best, and sublime service from the loveliest staff. Matchless. *Minimum stay two nights at weekends.*

Price	Half-board £220-£290 p.p. Suites £300-£600 p.p.
Rooms	24: 3 suites, 15 twins/doubles, 6 doubles.
Meals	Half-board only. Lunch £27-£41. Dinner for non-residents, £75-£85.
Closed	Never.
Directions	A30 west from Exeter to Whiddon Down. A382 south, then B3206 into Chagford. Right in square, right at fork. Signed straight across at x-roads.

Susan Kendall
Chagford TQ13 8HH

Tel 01647 432367
Web www.gidleigh.com

The Gate House

A dear house in a dear village, grander inside than you might think. The medieval longhouse (1460) has all the low beams and wonky walls you could hope for, and is properly looked after. Rose-print curtains and spruce quilts in the bedrooms, a wood-burner and flowers in the sitting room – and robes, good soaps and soft towels... such care is taken you can't help but feel spoiled. John and Sheila are delightful attentive hosts who serve you delicious Aga-side meals on white linen with candles. A small pool in the gardens overlooks beautiful woodland and moors; you may not want to leave.

Price	£72-£78. Singles £50.
Rooms	3: 2 twins/doubles; 1 double with separate bath/shower.
Meals	Supper trays £12.50. BYO. Packed lunch available. Pub/restaurant 50 yds.
Closed	Rarely.
Directions	From Moretonhampstead via Pound St to North Bovey (1.5 miles). House 25 yds off village green, down Lower Hill past inn on left.

John & Sheila Williams
North Bovey TQ13 8RB

Tel 01647 440479
Web www.gatehouseondartmoor.co.uk

Vogwell Cottage

Utter stillness pervades the valley. All you hear when you open your window are birdsong and brook – and the occasional chug-chug of the tractor. John and Christina have extended the old gamekeeper's cottage to create this cosy, unpretentious, woodland retreat. Your bedroom is old-fashioned and cottagey, light and airy with its own tiny wainscotted bathroom, the shared sitting room has books, board games (no TV here!) and open fire, and there's a sun room to loll around in. Come for the setting, delightful birdsong, great walking, delicious country cooking, the friendly dogs and the much-loved hens.

Price	£60. Singles £30.
Rooms	1 twin/double.
Meals	Dinner, 4 courses, £25. Supper £15. Packed lunch £5. Full-board available. Pubs 4 miles.
Closed	Christmas.
Directions	From Bovey Tracey signs to Manaton & Becky Falls; straight on past Kestor Inn in Manaton for 3.3 miles, following signs to Moretonhampstead. On left down lane.

John & Christina Everett
Manaton TQ13 9XD

Tel 01647 221302
Web www.vogwellcottage.co.uk

Easdon Cottage

Replenish your soul in this light and beautifully proportioned cottage; if the charming big double in the house is taken, you may stay in the nearby Barn (see opposite). Both have tranquillity and delightful moor views. The interiors are an enchanting mix of good pictures, oriental rugs, books, plants and some handsome Victorian finds. You are in a classic Devon valley yet the wilderness of Dartmoor lies just beyond the door, and the sweet cottage garden is filled with birds. Liza and Hugh's veggie and vegan breakfasts are imaginative and delicious. *Children & pets by arrangement.*

Price	From £65. Singles from £30.
Rooms	1 twin/double.
Meals	Supper £10-£20. Packed lunch £5. Pub/restaurant 3 miles.
Closed	Rarely.
Directions	A38 from Exeter; A382 for Bovey Tracey. There, left at 2nd r'bout for Manaton; 2 miles beyond Manaton, right at x-roads for M'hampstead. 0.5 miles on, right, signed Easdon. On left up track.

Liza & Hugh Dagnall
Long Lane, Manaton TQ13 9XB
Tel 01647 221389
Email easdondown@btopenworld.com

The Barn, Easdon Cottage

Difficult not to use the word 'hideaway': the setting is magical, secluded and entirely peaceful... sit and watch the sun go down from your little terraced garden. Hugh and Liza have converted with solid good taste: pine floors and good modern rugs, a corner kitchen cleverly fitted out, and maximum use of space. There's a Rayburn for winter warmth, a wicker sofa, a double futon to sprawl on and gorgeous views to the moors. The bathroom is cork-tiled, the double bed is king-size, a brocade curtain hugs the door for cosiness on winter nights, and the bedspread comes from Anokhi – an Indian touch.

Price	£215-£375 per week.
Rooms	Cottage for 2-3 (1 double & futon; 1 bath).
Meals	Restaurants/pubs within 10-minute drive.
Closed	Occasionally.
Directions	Directions given on booking.

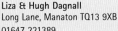

Liza & Hugh Dagnall
Long Lane, Manaton TQ13 9XB
Tel 01647 221389
Email easdondown@btopenworld.com

Lydgate House

You're in 36 acres of heaven. Herons dive in the river by day; you may get a glimpse from the conservatory as you dig into your bacon and eggs. The house is a dream, a nourishing stream of homely comforts: a drying room for walkers, deep white sofas, walls of books, a wood-burner and a cat in the armchair. Cindy, a classics teacher, and Peter, a surveyor, somehow find time to double up as host and hostess extraordinaire: expect a good chat, delicious home cooking and peace when you want it. Bedrooms – two are huge – are warmly cossetting: crisply floral with comfy beds and Radox in the bathrooms.

Price	£110-£140. Singles £50-£65.
Rooms	7: 4 doubles, 1 twin/double, 2 singles.
Meals	Dinner, 3 courses, £28.50.
Closed	January.
Directions	From Exeter A30 west to Whiddon Down, A382 south to Moretonhampstead, B3212 west to Postbridge. In village, left at pub. House signed straight ahead.

Cindy & Peter Farrington
Postbridge, Newton Abbot PL20 6TJ

Tel 01822 880209
Web www.lydgatehouse.co.uk

Bagtor House

What a setting! A ten-minute walk and you're on the moor. Enfolded by garden, green fields and sheep, the 15th-century house with the Georgian façade is the last remaining manor in the parish. Find ancient beauty in granite flagstones, oak-panelled walls, great fireplaces glowing with logs and country dressers brimming with china. Sue looks after hens, geese, labradors, guests, grows everything and makes her own bread. She offers you a large and elegant double room with an antique brass bed and, steeply up the stairs, a big attic-cosy suite perfect for families. Warm, homely, spacious, civilised.

Price	From £64. Singles by arrangement.
Rooms	2: 1 double, 1 family room, each with separate bath/shower.
Meals	Restaurants/pubs 1 mile.
Closed	Christmas.
Directions	From A38 to Plymouth, A382 turn off at r'bout, 3rd exit to Ilsington; up through village, 2nd left after hotel (to Bickington),1st crossroads right to Bagtor, 0.5 miles on, right next to Farm.

Sue Cookson
Ilsington, Newton Abbot TQ13 9RT

Tel 01364 661538
Web www.bagtormanor.co.uk

The Old Rectory

The lovely old house, surrounded by an organic cottage garden – with a twist – oozes tranquillity and calm. One of Rachel and Heather's hobbies is sculpture so although the decoration is traditional – wooden floors, pretty curtains, good furniture, family portraits – there are glimpses of well-travelled bohemianism. The dining room is iron-oxide red, there are tapestries from Ecuador and Peru, and vibrant colours glow in comfortable bedrooms. Pretty bathrooms sparkle with unusual tiles and original ceramic sinks, and there are long views from deep window seats. Charmingly relaxing and easy-going.

Price	From £60.
Rooms	2: 1 double; 1 family room with separate bath & shower.
Meals	Pubs within 0.25 miles.
Closed	November–March.
Directions	From A38 Exeter to Plymouth road towards Bovey Tracey. Follow signs to Widecombe, opposite post office.

Rachel Belgrave & Heather Garner
Widecombe in the Moor TQ13 7TB

Tel 01364 621231
Email rachel.belgrave@care4free.net

Corndonford Farm

An ancient Devon longhouse and an engagingly chaotic haven run by warm and friendly Ann and Will, along with their Shire horses and Dartmoor ponies. Steep, stone circular stairs lead to bedrooms; bright walls, a four poster with lacy curtains, gorgeous views over the cottage garden and a bathroom with a beam to duck. A place for those who want to get into the spirit of it all – maybe help catch an escaped foal, chatter to the farm workers around the table; not for fussy types or Mr and Mrs Tickety Boo. Good for walkers too – the Two Moors Way footpath is on the doorstep. *Children over ten by arrangement.*

Price	£56. Singles £33.
Rooms	2: 1 twin, 1 four-poster sharing bath.
Meals	Pub 2 miles.
Closed	Christmas.
Directions	From A38 2nd Ashburton turn for Dartmeet & Princetown. In Poundsgate pass pub on left; 3rd right on bad bend signed Corndon. Straight over x-roads, 0.5 miles, farm on left.

Ann & Will Williams
Poundsgate, Newton Abbot TQ13 7PP
Tel 01364 631595
Email corndonford@btinternet.com

Penpark

Clough Williams-Ellis of Portmeirion fame did more than design an elegant house; he made sure it communed with nature. Light pours in from every window, and the enchanting woodland garden and farmland views lift the spirits. The big double has apricot walls, a comfy sofa and its own balcony; the private suite has arched French doors to the garden and an extra room for young children. Antiques and heirlooms, African carvings, silk and fresh flowers – it is deeply traditional and comforting. Your generous hosts have been doing B&B for years and look after you so well.

Price	From £70. Singles by arrangement.
Rooms	3: 1 family suite; 1 twin/double with separate bath; 1 double with separate shower.
Meals	Pub 1 mile.
Closed	Rarely.
Directions	A38 west to Plymouth; A382 turn off; 3rd turning off r'bout, for Bickington. There, right at junc. (to Plymouth), right again (to Sigford & Widecombe). Over top of A38 & up hill; 1st entrance on right.

Madeleine & Michael Gregson
Bickington, Newton Abbot TQ12 6LH

Tel 01626 821314
Web www.penpark.co.uk

Hooks Cottage

The hideaway miner's cottage may have few original features but the setting is special. At the end of a long bumpy track is a lush oasis carved out of woodland. Mary, gently spoken, and Dick have a finely judged sense of humour, and labrador Archie will charm you. It is simple, rural, close to the Moors, with river and birdsong to unwind stressed souls. Carpeted bedrooms have a faded floral charm and pretty stream views; bathrooms are plain. Enjoy local sausages and Mary's marmalade for breakfast, the garden with horses, bluebells in spring, a swimming pool and 12 acres to explore.

Price	£50-£60. Singles from £30.
Rooms	2: 1 double, 1 twin.
Meals	Occasional supper, £15. Pub/restaurant 2 miles.
Closed	Rarely.
Directions	From A38, A382 at Drumbridges for Newton Abbot; 3rd left at r'bout for Bickington. Down hill, right for Haytor. Under bridge, 1st left & down long, bumpy track, past thatched cottage to house.

Mary & Dick Lloyd-Williams
Bickington, Ashburton TQ12 6JS

Tel 01626 821312
Email hookscottage@yahoo.com

Tudor House

A merchant's townhouse now happily given over to rooms for the Agaric Restaurant. Sophie and Nick are young, fun and very clever: in these mostly large, individually styled rooms, fabrics are plush, colours innovative and bathrooms have roll tops or a wet room style shower. A breakfast room is cool with leather and palms; full English or anything else you want is delivered here. Don't come without booking into the restaurant for fabulous modern British cooking – then stagger two steps down the street to your well-earned bed. Ashburton bustles with good food shops, antiques and books.

Price	£75-£125. Singles £50.
Rooms	5: 2 doubles, 1 family, 1 single; 1 double with separate bath.
Meals	Owner's restaurant next door. Packed lunch from £10 for 2.
Closed	Rarely.
Directions	From A38 follow signs to Ashburton. North Street is main street, house on right after Town Hall.

Sophie & Nick Coiley
36 North Street, Ashburton TQ13 7QD

Tel 01364 654478
Web www.agaricrestaurant.co.uk

Bickley Mill

A small inn full of good things. David and Tricia recently orchestrated a total refurbishment and their stylishly cosy interiors are just the ticket. Come for wood floors, stone walls, hessian rugs, cushioned sofas. Three fires burn in winter, there are Swedish benches, colourful art and a panelled breakfast room in creamy yellow. Bedrooms have a simple beauty in warm colours, pretty pine, trim carpets, crisp white linen. Downstairs you'll find helpful staff, local ales and loads of good food, from a light bite to a three-course feast – and a menu for children. A very generous place.

Price	£70-£80. Singles £55.
Rooms	8: 5 doubles, 2 twins, 1 family.
Meals	Lunch from £5. Dinner from £11.
Closed	Rarely.
Directions	South from Newton Abbot on A381. Left at garage in Ipplepen. Left at T-junc. after 1 mile. Down hill, left again, pub on left.

David & Tricia Smith
Stoneycombe, Kingskerswell TQ12 5LN

Tel 01803 873201
Web www.bickleymill.co.uk

Kingston House

"It's like visiting a National Trust home where you can get into bed," says Elizabeth, your gentle, erudite host. Set in a flawless Devon valley, Kingston is one of the finest surviving examples of early 18th-century English architecture: numerous open fires, murals peeling off the walls, a sitting room in the old chapel (look for the drunken cherubs) and 24 chimneys; the bed in the Green room has stood there since 1830. The cooking is historic, too – devilled kidneys, syllabub and proper trifle. Flowers by the thousand in various gardens and a small pool with a jet stream so you can swim 20 miles.

Price	£160-£180. Singles £100-£110.
Rooms	3: 2 doubles; 1 double with separate bath.
Meals	Lunch from £18.50. Dinner, 3 courses, £35. On request.
Closed	Christmas & New Year.
Directions	From A38, A384 to Staverton. At Sea Trout Inn, left fork for Kingston; halfway up hill right fork; at top, ahead at x-roads. Road goes up, then down to house; right to front of house.

Michael & Elizabeth Corfield
Staverton, Totnes TQ9 6AR

Tel 01803 762235
Web www.kingston-estate.co.uk

Kingston House Cottages

Bass Court, beautifully converted from a 1650 farm building, has a wood-burner in its inglenook, a galleried landing above, three super bedrooms and a Canadian hot tub in its private courtyard. Your thatched home is one of several on the estate of Kingston House so you can breakfast in the big house or be seduced by the home-cooked, home-produced meals brought to your door. Furnishings are the best of traditional, kitchens have all you need, beds are beautifully dressed and bathrooms have the thickest towels. A cream tea on arrival – a typical touch from generous hosts – and acres of garden to roam.

Price	£373-£1,518 per week.
Rooms	Little Shippen for 2. Jackdaws & The Old Stables for 4. Bass Court for 6.
Meals	Restaurants/pubs within 20-minute walk.
Closed	Never.
Directions	From A38, A384 to Staverton. At Sea Trout Inn, left fork for Kingston; halfway up hill right fork; at top, ahead at x-roads. Road goes up, then down to house; right to front of house.

Michael & Elizabeth Corfield
Staverton, Totnes TQ9 6AR

Tel 01803 762235
Web www.kingston-estate.co.uk

Manor Farm

Capable Sarah is a fanatical gardener, and produces vegetables that will find their way into your (excellent) dinner, and raspberries for your muesli. She keeps bees and hens too, so there's honey and eggs for breakfast, served in a smart red dining room. The farmhouse twists and turns around unexpected corners thanks to ancient origins, and the good-sized bedrooms, one with its own bathroom, both painted light yellow, are reached via two separate stairs – nicely private. The lovely village is surrounded by apple orchards and has two good pubs for eating out.

Price	£70. Singles £35.
Rooms	2: 1 double; 1 twin with separate bath/shower.
Meals	Dinner £15-£21. Packed lunch £4-£5. Pubs 500 yds.
Closed	Rarely.
Directions	From Newton Abbot, A381 for Totnes. After approx. 2.5 miles, right for Broadhempston. Past village sign, down hill & 2nd left. Pass pub on right & left 170 yds on into courtyard.

Sarah Clapp
Broadhempston, Totnes TQ9 6BD
Tel 01803 813260
Email mandsclapp@btinternet.com

Parliament House

The ancient rambling house (where William of Orange held his first Parliament) is on the road at the bottom of the valley, and has been beautifully restored by two designers. This is a fresh, stylish and charming cottage where wallpapers, napkins and toile de Jouy are to Carole's own design. White walls and serene colours form a lovely backdrop for pretty touches. Breakfasts are feasts – creamy mushrooms on a toasted muffin, three sorts of bread – and bedrooms are low-ceilinged and cosy with cast-iron fireplaces and hand-stencilled paper. There's a sitting room and a library with a piano – and the garden is a joy.

Price	From £75.
Rooms	2: 1 double; 1 twin/double with separate bath/shower.
Meals	Pubs/restaurants within 2 miles.
Closed	Rarely.
Directions	From Totnes, A385 Paignton road; 2 miles on, right at Riviera Sports Cars. House 1st on right. Just past house to parking area on right.

Carole & Harry Grimley
Longcombe, Totnes TQ9 6PR
Tel 01803 840288
Email parliamenthouse@btopenworld.com

Avenue Cottage

The tree-lined approach is steep and spectacular; the cottage sits in 11 wondrous acres of rhododendron, magnolia and wild flowers with a lily-strewn pond and paths that dip down towards the lovely river. Find a quiet spot in which to read or simply sit and absorb the tranquillity. Richard is a gifted gardener, and the archetypal gardener's modesty and calm have penetrated the house itself – it is sombre, uncluttered, comfortable. The old-fashioned twin room has a big bathroom with a faux-marble basin and a balcony with sweeping valley views; the pretty village and pub are a short walk away.

Price	£56-£70. Singles from £33.
Rooms	2: 1 twin/double; 1 double sharing shower.
Meals	Pub in village.
Closed	Rarely.
Directions	A381 Totnes-Kingsbridge for 1 mile; left for Ashprington; into village, then left by pub ('Dead End' sign). House 0.25 miles on right.

Richard Pitts
Ashprington, Totnes TQ9 7UT
Tel 01803 732769
Email richard.pitts@dial.pipex.com

Riverside House

The loveliest 17th-century cottage with wisteria and honeysuckle growing up its walls and the tidal river estuary bobbing past with boats and birds; in summer you can dip your toes in the water while sitting in the garden. Felicity, an artist, and Roger, a passionate sailor, give you beautiful bedrooms, fresh flowers, thick towels and pretty china. No need to stir from your fine linen-and-down nest to use the binoculars: bedrooms have long views over the water and wide windows. Wander up to the pub for dinner – in fine weather they have quayside barbecues and live music. *Minimum stay two nights at weekends.*

Price	From £70. Singles from £60.
Rooms	2: 1 double; 1 double with separate shower.
Meals	Packed lunch £6. Pubs 300 yds.
Closed	Rarely.
Directions	In Tuckenhay, pass Maltsters Arms on left to 2nd thatched house on left, at right angle to road. Drive past, turn at bridge and return to slip lane.

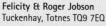

Felicity & Roger Jobson
Tuckenhay, Totnes TQ9 7EQ

Tel 01803 732837
Web www.riverside-house.co.uk

End Cottage

Beyond the very pretty front garden (Penny is a garden designer), the house, last in a terrace of three, faces south to the village. Inside, light pours into every room; curtains are ceiling-to-floor and the beds have beautiful linen; bathrooms are generous and up-to-date. The sitting room is big and cosy with a red sofa, log stoves, books and games, and there's more space for lounging in the charming farmhouse kitchen; this feels like staying in a friend's house. Step out to the pretty village of Cornworthy with its award-winning pub, or try one of the circular walks from the door. Perfect.

Price	£360-£850 per week.
Rooms	2 doubles; 1 twin; bath & shower room; bathroom.
Meals	Pub in village.
Closed	Never.
Directions	Directions given on booking.

Penny Smith
Mount Pleasant, Cornworthy, Totnes TQ9 7ES
Tel 020 8672 7617
Web www.endcottage.com

The Old Rectory

Fresh flowers and 18th-century elegance... the Regency rectory, on the edge of Diptford, was once the home of William Gregor, a vicar who discovered titanium! (There are still some titanium bowls in the large and lovely hall with its fine staircase.) You'll enjoy eating here, in the splendour of the dining room, for Jill is a superb, Leith-trained cook and a vivacious hostess. Bedrooms are all large and light; one is downstairs, another has three lovely windows with views over the romantic garden to the moors – and a chesterfield so you can appreciate them in comfort. Pets are exceedingly welcome.

Price	£85-£95. Singles £57.50.
Rooms	4: 2 doubles, 1 twin, 1 family suite for 4.
Meals	Dinner, 3 courses, £27.50. Pubs 2 miles.
Closed	Rarely.
Directions	Avonwick to Diptford road. First house on right after village sign.

Jill Hitchins
Diptford, Totnes TQ9 7NY

Tel 01548 821575
Web www.oldrectorydiptford.co.uk

Lower Norton Farmhouse

Hard to believe the downstairs bedroom was a calving pen and its smart bathroom the dairy. Now it has a seagrass floor and a French walnut bed. All Glynis's rooms are freshly decorated, and she and Peter are the most amenable hosts, genuinely happy for you to potter around all day should you wish to do so. For the more active, a yacht on the Dart and a cream Bentley are to hand, with Peter as navigator and chauffeur – rare treats. Return to gardens, paddocks, peaceful views, super dinners and a big log fire. Off the beaten track, a tremendous find. *Children over ten welcome.*

Price	From £70. Singles from £55.
Rooms	2 doubles, 1 twin.
Meals	Dinner, 2 courses, £20. Lunch £7.50. Packed lunch £6. Pub/restaurant 1.5 miles.
Closed	Rarely.
Directions	From A381 at Halwell, 3rd left signed Slapton; 4th right after 2.3 miles signed Valley Springs Fishery at Wallaton Cross. House down 3rd drive on left.

Peter & Glynis Bidwell
Coles Cross, East Allington, Totnes TQ9 7RL
Tel 01548 521246
Web www.lowernortonfarmhouse.co.uk

The White House

A great little place in a peaceful corner; gaze on the sparkling Dart estuary from the comfort of your deep bed. A maritime theme plays throughout this relaxing, book-filled home, and there's classical music at breakfast. Fresh and cheerful bedrooms have tea, coffee, sherry, chocolates, bathrobes and views; more panoramas from the wide garden terrace by the river. In winter the guest sitting/breakfast room is cosy with open fire, comfortable chairs, masses of books. A ferry transports you to Dartmouth and on to Totnes, and Hugh and Jill are gracious and generous hosts. *Children by arrangement.*

Price	£80. Singles £55.
Rooms	2 doubles.
Meals	Pubs a short walk.
Closed	Christmas.
Directions	Down hill into Dittisham, sharp right immed. before Red Lion. Along The Level, up narrow hill & house entrance opp. at junc. of Manor St & Rectory Lane.

Hugh & Jill Treseder
Manor Street, Dittisham TQ6 0EX
Tel 01803 722355

Fingals

Don't come if you are stuffy. But I challenge any of you with an open mind and sense of fun to fail to enjoy Fingals. Is it a home or is it a hotel? Beautiful and stuffed with all the bits and pieces to make you happy and comfortable (inside pool, jacuzzi, sauna, grass tennis court, library, superbly comfortable rooms, etc) it throbs with the vitality and enthusiasm of both Richard and Sheila. Conversation, good food and wine flow loosely round the family dinner table and throughout the house. A smashing place... and there's even a stream flowing through the garden. *Minimum stay two nights at weekends.*

Price	£75-£160.
Rooms	10 + 1: 8 doubles, 1 twin, 1 family.
Meals	Dinner £30.
Closed	2 January-26 March.
Directions	From Totnes, A381 south; left for Cornworthy. Right at x-roads for Cornworthy; right at ruined gatehouse for Dittisham. Down steep hill, over bridge. Signed on right.

Richard & Sheila Johnston
Dittisham, Dartmouth TQ6 0JA
Tel 01803 722398
Web www.fingals.co.uk

Fingals Barn

Lying in a rolling valley half a mile from the River Dart, the Barn is part of a hotel (fun, quirky, laid back) so everything you need is on the spot (pool, snooker, tennis, restaurant). The new oak-framed Barn is a huge open space with massive beams, floor-to-ceiling windows, comfortable sofas and interesting pictures. The basic open-plan kitchen is at one end, and the main bedroom with sloping roof and skylight windows on the other side of a sliding Japanese screen. There's a second, much smaller bedroom just right for children and a bathroom with a green-footed roll-top bath. *Pets welcome by arrangement.*

Price	£400-£800 per week.
Rooms	Barn for 4 (1 double, 1 twin; bath/shower).
Meals	Dittisham 20-minute walk.
Closed	Never.
Directions	From Totnes, A381 south; left for Cornworthy. Right at x-roads for Cornworthy; right at ruined gatehouse for Dittisham. Down steep hill, over bridge. Signed on right.

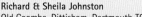

Richard & Sheila Johnston
Old Coombe, Dittisham, Dartmouth TQ6 0JA

Tel 01803 722398
Web www.fingals.co.uk

Nonsuch House

The photo says it all! You are in your own crow's nest, perched above the flotillas of yachts zipping in and out of the estuary mouth: stunning. Kit and Penny are great fun and look after you well; Kit is an ex-hotelier, smokes his own fish fresh from the quay and knocks out brilliant dinners, bedrooms are big and comfortably floral, fresh bathrooms sparkle. Breakfasts on the terrace or in the conservatory are a delight and views sweep over the river and out to sea. Further pleasures lie across the water: a five-minute walk brings you to the ferry that transports you and your car to the other side. *Children over ten welcome. Minimum stay two nights at weekends.*

Price	£95-£125. Singles £70-£100.
Rooms	4: 3 twins/doubles, 1 double.
Meals	Dinner, 3 courses, £27.50. (Not Tues/Wed/Sat.) Pub/restaurant 5-minute walk & short boat trip.
Closed	Rarely.
Directions	2 miles before Brixham on A3022, A379. After r'bout, fork left (B3205) downhill, through woods, left up Higher Contour Rd, down Ridley Hill. At hairpin bend.

Kit & Penny Noble
Church Hill, Kingswear, Dartmouth TQ6 0BX

Tel 01803 752829
Web www.nonsuch-house.co.uk

Knocklayd

Built in 1905, this family house makes the most of its extraordinary views of the estuary and harbour; the sitting rooms and pretty bedrooms each take a different angle, and there are peaceful places to sit in the garden and watch the colourful scene below. Inside find softly coloured fabrics, carpets and wallpapers, and lots of family furniture, prints and paintings. Jonathan was a naval attaché so you're beautifully looked after. Boating can be arranged, trains met, nothing is too much trouble. And for breakfast? Locally smoked haddock, salmon and scrambled eggs, homemade jams, compotes and smoothies.

Price	£80. Singles £50.
Rooms	3: 2 doubles, 1 twin/double.
Meals	Supper & dinner from £20. Pub/restaurant 400 yds.
Closed	Rarely.
Directions	To Kingswear on B3205, left fork for Kingswear and Lower Ferry. Down hill, 1 mile, road climbs and becomes one way. Fork left into Higher Contour Road, half mile on left into Redoubt Hill; park by second gate; signed.

Susan & Jonathan Cardale
Redoubt Hill, Kingswear TQ6 0DA

Tel 01803 752873
Web www.knocklayd.com

Browns Hotel

Bang in the centre of bustling Dartmouth: a large, airy space with vibrant paintings on cream and lilac walls, cast-iron fireplaces and squashy sofas; park here and ponder which of the fresh tapas dishes to order. James has his pick of Devon's finest fish, meat and veg, so your taste buds will be thrilled. Bedrooms vary in size – none are huge – but all have pocket-sprung mattresses, plain colours with the odd funky headboard or zebra-striped screen, super snazzy bathrooms and modern art. Gorgeous breakfasts, fantastic cocktails, board games for rainy days, sailing for sunny ones. *Minimum stay two nights at weekends.*

Price	£85-£170. Singles £65 (Sunday-Thursday).
Rooms	10: 8 doubles, 1 twin, 1 four-poster.
Meals	Tapas £3.50-£8 (Thursday-Saturday only).
Closed	January.
Directions	From M5, A38 for Plymouth; A385 for Totnes then to Dartmouth. There, 3rd right (Townstal Road) & down into town. On right hand side.

James & Clare Brown
27-29 Victoria Road, Dartmouth TQ6 9RT

Tel 01803 832572
Web www.brownshoteldartmouth.co.uk

Greenswood Farm

A lovely, low Devon longhouse covered in wisteria, with stone flagging, deep window sills, and elegant furniture. The garden is large, south-facing and completely sheltered; admire the three ponds, the perfect beds and borders. But this is a working farm and there is no stuffiness in Helen and Roger – you will find a warm and cosy place to relax and enjoy the gorgeous valley. Bedrooms are feminine but not namby-pamby and old pine chests give a solid feel. Organic beef and lamb are reared on the farm and breakfast eggs come straight from Sally Henny Penny outside; buy some to take home.

Price	From £75. Singles by arrangement.
Rooms	3: 2 doubles, 1 twin.
Meals	Dinner (min. 4) by arrangement. Pubs/restaurants 3 miles.
Closed	Rarely.
Directions	A381 for Dartmouth. At Golf & Country Club right to Strete. Signpost after 1 mile.

Mrs Helen Baron
Greenswood Lane, Dartmouth TQ6 0LY

Tel 01803 712100
Web www.greenswood.co.uk

Woodside Cottage

From a narrow decorative window, a charming vignette of Devon: a winding lane edged by fat hedgerows, a cow-dotted hillside. The 18th-century former gamekeeper's cottage is folded into Devon's gentle green softness. Bedrooms are comfortable, the drawing and dining rooms formal and immaculate. Tim and Sally welcome you with tea and homemade cake; breakfast on homemade bread and muesli, with eggs from neighbouring hens. An excellent gastropub, the sea and moors are all near; at night see the beam from Start Point lighthouse. *Minimum stay two nights (except November-March).*

Price	From £75. Singles by arrangement.
Rooms	3: 2 doubles, 1 twin/double.
Meals	Packed lunch £5. Half-board option with dinner & wine at village pub.
Closed	Christmas.
Directions	A381 from Totnes to Halwell, A3122 for Dartmouth. After Dartmouth Golf Club, right at sign to house & Blackawton; 0.3 miles before Blackawton, cottage on right.

Tim & Sally Adams
Blackawton, Dartmouth TQ9 7BL

Tel 01803 898164
Web www.woodsidedartmouth.co.uk

Hazelwood House

Hazelwood isn't your standard hotel or B & B, it's a country venue with accommodation for all who wish to rest, retreat and recoup – you may occasionally find yourself among guests on a residential course. It's a comfy, no frills house with open fires, sublime peace and a large drawing and dining room. Bedrooms are homely with an assortment of furniture, some have huge views over the valley, some face the back. Cream teas on the wisteria-shaded veranda are wonderful and you get lectures, exhibitions, courses, even recitals. Wellington boots wait at the front door, there's a boathouse on the river.

Price	£70-£150. Singles £47-£112.
Rooms	15: 4 doubles, 2 twins, 1 family room, all en suite; 2 doubles, 2 twins, 2 family rooms, 1 single, sharing 4 baths.
Meals	Lunch £14. Dinner £30-£35.
Closed	Never.
Directions	From Exeter, A38 south; A3121 south. Left onto B3196 south. At California Cross, 1st left after petrol station. After 0.75 miles, left.

Janie Bowman, Gillian Kean & Anabel Watson
Loddiswell, Kingsbridge TQ7 4EB

Tel 01548 821232
Web www.hazelwoodhouse.com

Lower Coombe Royal, The Garden Rooms & Coach House

Susi and Paul are passionate about their eight-acre restoration project in the beautiful South Hams. The Garden Rooms is perfect for two: an open-plan living area with solid oak floors, wood-burning stove, smart cream kitchen, Italianate terrace. On the same floor is the bedroom, its fabulous big bed clad in cream organic cotton. The Coach House is completely hidden away and great for families, with space and a huge terrace for outdoor fun. Both properties are eco-friendly and surrounded by gardens with treehouses and rhododendrons; welcome treats include Paul's homemade bread.

Price	Garden Rooms £530-£1,030. Coach House £740-£1,680. Prices per week.
Rooms	Garden Rooms for 2. Coach House for 6.
Meals	Restaurant/pub within 10-minute walk.
Closed	Rarely.
Directions	Directions given on booking.

Susi & Paul Titchener
Kingsbridge TQ7 4AD
Tel 01548 852880
Web www.lowercoomberoyal.co.uk

Buckland Tout-Saints

Tiny lanes lead up to this William and Mary manor house – the land was listed in the Domesday book – and the dovecote is one of England's oldest. Inside you find grandly panelled reception rooms dressed in shimmering Russian pine. There's a bar in red leather, a ceiling rose in the stately dining room, a terrace with big views for afternoon tea. First-floor bedrooms come in country-house style: high ceilings, warm colours, fine views. Those above in the eaves are smaller but funkier, with neutral colours, flat-screen TVs, comfy beds. Excellent food is often organic, and Salcombe and Dartmouth are both close.

Price	£135-£225. Suites from £245. Singles from £95.
Rooms	16: 12 doubles, 2 twins, 2 suites.
Meals	Lunch from £7.50. Dinner, 3 courses, about £35.
Closed	Never.
Directions	A381 south from Totnes for Kingsbridge. Hotel signed right three miles south of Halwell. Follow signs up narrow lanes to hotel.

Howard Turner
Goveton, Kingsbridge TQ7 2DS

Tel 01548 853055
Web www.tout-saints.co.uk

Washbrook Barn

Hard not to feel happy here – even the blue-painted windows on rosy stone walls make you want to smile. Inside is equally sunny. The barn – decrepit until Penny bought it four years ago – rests at the bottom of a quiet valley. She has transformed it into a series of big light-filled rooms with polished wooden floors, pale beams and richly coloured walls lined with fabulous watercolours: the effect is one of gaiety and panache. No sitting room as such, but armchairs in impeccable bedrooms from which one can admire the view. The beds are divinely comfortable and the fresh bathrooms sparkle.

Price	£70-£75. Singles £50.
Rooms	3: 1 double; 1 double, 1 twin, each with separate bath/shower.
Meals	Dinner occasionally available in winter. Pubs/restaurants 10-minute walk.
Closed	Christmas & New Year.
Directions	Kingsbridge quay to top of Fore St; right to Duncombe St; left to Church St. Right to Belle Cross Rd; right to Washbrook Lane; left fork; on right.

Penny Cadogan
Washbrook Lane, Kingsbridge TQ7 1NN

Tel 01548 856901
Web www.washbrookbarn.co.uk

West Charleton Grange

The approach is charming and this is bliss for families: Wendy house and play areas, short tennis court and indoor heated pool, cricket bats and games and a secret garden among the apple trees. Wisely, each holiday home has its living room upstairs to make the most of the views; most have wood-burners; five have private patios. Kitchens are new, with black granite worktops and every mod con, bathrooms sport Heritage suites, beds are luxuriously comfy; fresh flowers and wine greet you on arrival. Amazing beaches are a short drive – and the village shop is so close the kids can pick up the bread.

Price	£575-£2,045 per week.
Rooms	West Wing for 6; 5 cottages for 2-6.
Meals	Pub within 10-minute walk.
Closed	Rarely.
Directions	Directions given on booking.

Hazel Bustin
West Charleton, Kingsbridge TQ7 2AD
Tel 01548 531779
Web www.westcharletongrange.com

Seabreeze

Seabreeze is a treat. Small, cute and nicely relaxed, a little piece of homespun magic. It's not grand, but what you get is priceless. Andrew organises kite surfing, Charlotte runs the café. There are kayaks and bikes for intrepid adventures, cliff walks for fabulous views. Airy interiors are just as they should be: colourful and comfy. You get stripped floors, halogen lighting, sky-blue tongue and groove panelling. Bedrooms are perfect for the price: crisp linen, seaside colours, flat-screen TVs, super bathrooms, two have sea views. Fabulous seafood at the Start Bay Inn is yards away. *Minimum stay two nights at weekends.*

Price	£60-£100. Singles from £40.
Rooms	3: 1 double, 1 twin/double, 1 family.
Meals	Lunch (March-October) from £5. Restaurants in village.
Closed	Rarely.
Directions	A379 south from Dartmouth to Torcross. House on seafront in village.

Andrew & Charlotte Barker
Torcross, Kingsbridge TQ7 2TQ

Tel	01548 580697
Web	www.seabreezebreaks.com

Rafters Barn

A delightful and peaceful 300-year-old barn along the narrowest of lanes and with soaring views down a valley to the sea. This is big sailing country but mostly agricultural so you will avoid the madding crowds. You have a comfy guest sitting room with big sofas and a wood-burner that belts out the heat, neat bedrooms in bright colours with pretty touches, tiled bathrooms that gleam and a great big breakfast in the open hallway. Elizabeth is thoughtful and smiley and will point you to the best beaches and places to eat in Salcombe. Or let her cook for you – with produce fresh from farmers' markets.

Price	£65. Singles £40.
Rooms	3: 1 double, 1 twin; 1 single with separate bath.
Meals	Dinner £15. Pubs/restaurants 4 miles.
Closed	Christmas & New Year.
Directions	A381 dir. Salcombe. Just before Hope Cove sign, right to Bagton & S. Huish. Follow lane for 1 mile; 30 yds past saw mill, right up farm lane; at bottom on left.

Elizabeth Hanson
Holwell Farm, South Huish, Kingsbridge TQ7 3EQ

Tel 01548 560460
Web www.raftersdevon.co.uk

The Henley

A small house above the sea with fabulous views and some of the loveliest food in Devon. Warm interiors come with stripped wood floors, seagrass matting: beyond, the Avon estuary slips out to sea and at high tide surfers ride the waves; at low tide you can walk on the sands. There's a pretty garden with a path down to the sea, binoculars in each room, a wood-burner in the snug and good books everywhere. Bedrooms are not large but in warm yellows with crisp linen, tongue-and-groove panelling and robes in super little bathrooms. As for Martyn's table d'hôte dinners, expect something special. *Minimum stay two nights at weekends.*

Price	£100-£120. Singles from £60.
Rooms	5: 3 doubles, 2 twins/doubles.
Meals	Dinner £29.
Closed	November-March.
Directions	From A38, A3121 to Modbury, then B3392 to Bigbury-on-Sea. Hotel on left as road slopes down to sea.

Martyn Scarterfield & Petra Lampe
Folly Hill, Bigbury-on-Sea TQ7 4AR

Tel 01548 810240
Web www.thehenleyhotel.co.uk

Burgh Island

Burgh is unique – grand English Art Deco, and much more than a hotel – you come to join a cast of players – so bring your pearls and get ready for cocktails under a stained-glass dome. By day you lie on steamers in the garden or try your hand at a game of croquet. At night you dress for dinner, sip vermouth in a palm-fringed bar, then shuffle off to the ballroom and dine on delicious organic food while the sounds of swing and jazz fill the air. Art Deco bedrooms are the real thing: Bakerlite telephones, ancient radios, bowls of fruit and panelled walls. There's snooker, tennis, massage, a sauna. *Minimum stay two nights at weekends.*

Price	Half-board £320-£340. Suites £380-£500.
Rooms	24: 10 doubles, 3 twins, 12 suites.
Meals	Half-board only. Lunch £10-£38. Dinner for non-residents, 3 courses, £55.
Closed	Rarely.
Directions	Drive to Bigbury-on-Sea. At high tide you are transported by sea tractor, at low tide by Landrover. Walking takes three minutes.

Deborah Clark & Tony Orchard
Bigbury-on-Sea TQ7 4BG

Tel 01548 810514
Web www.burghisland.com

Orchard Cottage

Tucked into a quiet village corner, this is the last cottage in a row of three. Walk through the pretty garden, past seats that (sometimes!) bask in the sun and down to your own entrance and terrace… you may come and go as you please. Your bedroom is L-shaped and large, with a comfortable brass bed and a super en suite shower; it is spotless yet rustic. The Ewens are friendly and fun, their two spaniels equally so and you are brilliantly sited for Dartmoor, Plymouth, the sand and the sea. Breakfasts in the beamed dining room are generous and delicious; this is excellent value B&B.

Price	£50. Singles £35.
Rooms	1 double.
Meals	Pubs 300 yds.
Closed	Christmas.
Directions	A379 from Plymouth for Modbury. On reaching Church St at top of hill, before Modbury, fork left at Palm Cross, then 1st right by school into Back St. Cottage 3rd on left, past village hall.

Maureen Ewen
Back Street, Palm Cross Green, Modbury PL21 0QZ
Tel 01548 830633
Email moewen@talktalk.net

South Hooe Count House

Heavenly peace to do your own thing in this little cottage by the Tamar. The walls of the bedroom and sitting room are panelled with the original wood and both have deep window seats from where you can watch the ever changing light reflected in the water. Cook your own breakfast whenever you want on the Rayburn: homemade bread and marmalade, eggs from the hens. Warm yourself by the wood-burner then sleep peacefully; footsteps in the night are likely to be Martha's, the friendly donkey who grazes nearby. A steep path leads down to the shore – borrow a canoe and paddle up stream to explore, then float home with the tide. *Minimum stay 3 nights.*

Price	£80.
Rooms	1 double/twin.
Meals	Pub 3 miles.
Closed	Rarely.
Directions	Into Bere Alston on B3257, left for Weir Quay. Over x-roads. Follow Hole's Hole sign, right for Hooe. Fork left for South Hooe Farm; 300 yds on, turn sharply back to your left & down track.

Trish Dugmore
Hole's Hole, Bere Alston, Yelverton PL20 7BW
Tel 01822 840329
Email southhooe@aol.com

The Horn of Plenty

This country-house hotel, in five acres of silence, has been thrilling guests for 40 years. Airy interiors are the essence of graceful simplicity with stripped floors, gilt mirrors, exquisite art and flowers everywhere. Bedrooms elate with painted wooden floors, shimmering throws or crushed velvet headboards; all come fully armed with an excess of hi-tech gadgetry, bathrooms are predictably divine. Try foie gras crème brûlée, loin of venison with spiced pear, then chocolate truffle mousse with raspberry sauce. In summer you can eat on the terrace with views of the Tamar in the valley below.

Price	£160-£250. Singles £150-£240.
Rooms	10 twins/doubles.
Meals	Lunch, 3 courses, £26.50. Dinner, 3 courses, £45.
Closed	25 & 26 December.
Directions	A386 north to Tavistock. Turn left onto A390, following signs to Callington. After 3 miles, right at Gulworthy Cross. Signed.

Paul Roston & Peter Gorton
Gulworthy, Tavistock PL19 8JD

Tel	01822 832528
Web	www.thehornofplenty.co.uk

Mount Tavy Cottage

Quiet and rural – but just a short walk to Tavistock (best market town 2005). Everything is geared to your comfort – pretty rooms, four-poster and half-tester beds, deep, free-standing baths. Joanna and Graham, a lovely Devon couple, have worked hard to restore this former gardener's bothy, Graham making much of the furniture himself. Two new bedrooms have been created in the potting shed across the courtyard; here you have complete independence. Outside are ponds – one with a breezy pagoda for summer suppers – and a walled Victorian garden filled with birds and wildlife.

Price	From £60. Singles from £30.
Rooms	3: 2 twins/doubles, 1 four-poster, each with separate bath.
Meals	Dinner, 3 courses, £20. Pub 2 miles.
Closed	Rarely.
Directions	From Tavistock B3357 towards Princetown; 0.25 miles on, after Mount House School, left. Drive past lake to house.

Mr & Mrs G H Moule
Tavistock PL19 9JL
Tel 01822 614253
Web www.mounttavy.co.uk

Browns Hotel

The house dates to 1700 and was Tavistock's first coaching inn. It's still the best place to stay in town, with armchairs in front of the fire, wood floors in the restaurant, and a stone-flagged conservatory for delicious breakfasts. Clutter-free bedrooms have a clipped elegance: Egyptian cotton, latticed windows and comforting bathrobes. Some in the coach house are huge, with cathedral ceilings. Dine under beams on Cornish scallops, roast lamb, rhubarb and custard crumble. Tavistock is an old market town, its famous goose fair takes place in October. Don't miss Dartmoor for uplifting walks.

Price	£110-£220. Singles from £70.
Rooms	20: 11 doubles, 3 twins, 6 singles.
Meals	Continental breakfast included. Cooked dishes £6.00-£12.50. Lunch from £9. Dinner £32-£37. 5-course tasting menu £45.
Closed	Never.
Directions	Leave A386 for Tavistock. Right, at statue, for town centre. Left at T-junction, them immediately left into West Street. Hotel on right. Ask about parking.

Helena King & Phil Biggin
80 West Street, Tavistock PL19 8AQ

Tel 01822 618686
Web www.brownsdevon.co.uk

Tor Cottage

Lavish, spoiling, decadent – Maureen's professionalism and desire to please means that nothing is left to chance and every detail of your stay is carefully thought out. Bedside truffles, fresh fruit, flowers, Cava and soft robes in neat, traditional bedrooms with open fireplaces and a private terrace or conservatory. Bathrooms, too, have all that you need. The garden is idyllic, full of secret corners, with fountains colourfully lit at night and paths and steps to guide you through the beauty; a stream runs by and the pool is heated. Breakfasts are served in the sunroom. *Minimum stay two nights. Special deals available.*

Price	£140-£150. Singles £94. Self-catering from £66 (min. 3 nights).
Rooms	5: 2 doubles, 1 twin/double, 1 suite; 1 woodland cabin for 2 (B&B or self-catering).
Meals	Supper, 3 courses, £24. On request.
Closed	B&B: Christmas & New Year. Self-catering: Never.
Directions	In Chillaton keep pub & PO on left, up hill towards Tavistock. After 300 yds, right down bridleway (ignore No Access signs).

Maureen Rowlatt
Chillaton, Tavistock PL16 0JE

Tel 01822 860248
Web www.torcottage.co.uk

Burnville House

Granite gateposts, Georgian house, rhododendrons, beechwoods and rolling fields of sheep: that's the setting. But there's more. Beautifully proportioned rooms reveal subtle colours, elegant antiques, squishy sofas and bucolic views, stylish bathrooms are sprinkled with candles, there are sumptuous dinners and pancakes at breakfast. Your hosts left busy jobs in London to settle here, and their place breathes life – space, smiles, energy. Swim, play tennis, walk to Dartmoor from the door, take a trip to Eden or the sea. Or... just gaze at the moors and the church on the Tor and listen to the silence, and the sheep.

Price	From £70. Singles £45.
Rooms	2 doubles.
Meals	Dinner from £15. Pub 2 miles.
Closed	Rarely.
Directions	A30 Exeter-Okehampton; A386 dir. Tavistock. Right for Lydford opp. Dartmoor Inn; after 4 miles (thro' Lydford), Burnville Farm on left (convex traffic mirror on right).

Victoria Cunningham
Brentor, Tavistock PL19 0NE

Tel 01822 820443
Web www.burnville.co.uk

The Dartmoor Inn

There aren't many inns where you can sink into Zoffany-clad winged armchairs in the dining room, snooze on a pink silk bed under a French chandelier, or shop for rhinestone brooches and Provençal quilts while you wait for dinner. Come also for stripped wood floors, timber-framed walls, sand-blasted settles and country-house rugs. Try Philip's ambrosial food (corned beef hash for breakfast, ham hock terrine for lunch, free-range duck for dinner) and sleep well in bedrooms with triple-glazed windows that defeat any road noise. The moors are on your doorstep, so walk in the wind, then eat, drink and sleep.

Price	£100-£115.
Rooms	3 doubles.
Meals	Lunch from £5. Dinner from £15.
Closed	Occasionally.
Directions	North from Tavistock on A386. Pub on right at Lydford turnoff.

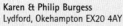

Karen & Philip Burgess
Lydford, Okehampton EX20 4AY

Tel 01822 820221
Web www.dartmoorinn.com

Lewtrenchard Manor

A thrilling, historical pastiche set in a Jacobean mansion; one fabulous room follows another until you reach the 1602 gallery, with the salvaged, honeycombed, plaster-moulded ceiling, grand piano and 1725 Bible. Bedrooms are large – Queen Henrietta Maria's four-poster sits in one of the traditional bedrooms in the main house; there's a more contemporary feel to the new North Wing rooms. A pretty inner courtyard is great for summer Sunday lunches (with jazz) and the food is as local and seasonal as possible – modern British style with a Mediterranean and Asian twist.

Price	£150-£250. Singles from £125.
Rooms	14: 9 doubles, 5 suites.
Meals	Lunch £15-£19 (not Monday). Dinner from £40.
Closed	Rarely.
Directions	From Exeter, exit A30 for A386. At T-junc., right, then 1st left for Lewdown. After 6 miles, left for Lewtrenchard. House signed left after 0.75 miles.

Jason Hornbuckle
Lewdown, Okehampton EX20 4PN

Tel 01566 783222
Web www.lewtrenchard.co.uk

Percy's Country Hotel

A gorgeous, 130-acre organic estate teeming with life: pigs roam freely through woodland, Jacob sheep graze, geese, ducks and chickens supply eggs for breakfast. There's a huge kitchen garden that's planted seasonally and, at the house, Tina turns her ingredients into soups and salads, terrines and sausages; a meal here is no ordinary event. Bedrooms in the converted granary are smart, with big comfortable beds, chic leather sofas, flat screen TVs and spotless bathrooms (some with whirlpools). Grab a pair of wellies and lose yourself in the estate – woodpeckers and kingfishers, deer and badger.

Price	£150-£210. Singles £155-£185. Half-board £115-£155 p.p.
Rooms	8 twins/doubles.
Meals	Dinner, 3 courses, £40.
Closed	Never.
Directions	From Okehampton, A3079 for Metherell Cross. After 8.3 miles, left. Hotel on left after 6.5 miles.

Tina & Tony Bricknell-Webb
Virginstow, Okehampton EX21 5EA

Tel 01409 211236
Web www.percys.co.uk

The Devon Wine School

Alastair and Carol run their wine school from this delightfully rural spot – and look after you to perfection. Chill out in an open-plan sitting/dining room with wooden floors, smart chesterfields, Xian terracotta warriors, claret walls and rolling views. Bedrooms are light, unfussy and elegant, bathrooms are swish, food is taken seriously and sourced locally (an organic beef farmer lives next door). The atmosphere is relaxed and friendly; the wine, obviously, is a joy – and reasonably priced! There's a hard tennis court for working up an appetite and no light pollution; star-gazers will be happy.

Price	£70. Singles £50.
Rooms	2: 1 twin/double, 1 double with child's room (no extra charge).
Meals	Dinner, 3 courses, from £20. Occasional lunch. Pub 1 mile.
Closed	Rarely.
Directions	From Cadeleigh, 1.5 miles to Postbox Cross, left to Cheriton Fitzpaine. Follow road to Redyeates Cross x-roads; right, house is 150 yds on left down track.

Alastair & Carol Peebles
Redyeates Farm, Cheriton Fitzpaine, Crediton EX17 4HG
Tel 01363 866742
Web www.devonwineschool.co.uk

West Bradley

Total immersion in beauty – doves in the farmyard, hens in the orchard, fields on either side of the long drive. Privacy, too, in your 18th-century upside-down barn on the side of the owners' Devon longhouse – and views. A handmade oak staircase, oak floors, two freshly furnished bedrooms (one up, one down), a good big sitting room with a gas-fired wood-burner and a kitchen you would be happy to use. Phillida can bring breakfast to you here, or you can tuck into full English in the farmhouse dining room. There will be homemade something on arrival and a good choice of local pubs.

Price	£80. Singles £50.
Rooms	2: 1 twin/double; 1 twin with separate shower. Guest kitchen.
Meals	Pubs within 5 miles.
Closed	Rarely.
Directions	B3137 Tiverton-Witheridge; on towards Rackenford & Calverleigh. After pink thatched cottage (2 miles), fork left to Templeton; West Bradley 2 miles; on left before village hall.

Martin & Phillida Strong
Templeton, Tiverton EX16 8BJ
Tel 01884 253220
Email martinstrong@westbradley.eclipse.co.uk

Bark House Hotel

A pretty, long old house, swathed in wisteria and sitting smartly by the main, but not busy, road. Martin and Melanie have newly taken over here and regulars may notice a few changes: the dining room has been lightened with fresh paint, white table cloths and pretty cream chairs, the drawing room has had similar treatment, but the attention to detail and the excellent service are still superb for a place this size. Bedrooms are not huge, except for one which has a fine bay window and its own door to the pretty garden, but all are pristine and comfortable with lovely views. Dinners are home-cooked and delicious, your hosts charming and helpful.

Price	£97-£128.
Rooms	5: 3 doubles, 2 twins/doubles.
Meals	Dinner £29.50.
Closed	Occasionally.
Directions	From Tiverton, A396 north towards Minehead. On right, 1 mile north of junction with B3227.

Melanie McKnight & Martin French
Oakfordbridge, Bampton EX16 9HZ

Tel	01398 351236
Web	www.barkhouse.co.uk

Staghound Cottages

Brilliant for walkers and cyclists: the cottage is a mile from Exmoor, near the Bristol to Padstow cycle route, and Penny – a potter whose work fills the house – has space for bikes and wet clothes. *And* there's a bus stop outside. Built as an inn several centuries ago (there's a still-functioning pub next door), it overlooks meadows and rolling hills. The interior is not luxurious but simple, calm and appealing; bedrooms, big and small, have wonky floors and beds with fresh cotton. No guest sitting room but you'll be out exploring all day and Penny will start you off with a great breakfast.

Price	£45-£55. Singles £25.
Rooms	3: 1 double; 1 twin/double, 1 single sharing bath/shower.
Meals	Packed lunch £4. Restaurants 2 miles.
Closed	Christmas.
Directions	M5 exit 27 for Tiverton; 7 miles, right at r'bout for Dulverton; left at next r'bout. At Black Cat junc. take middle road to Dulverton; in Exebridge, left at round house; 300 yds on left.

Penny Richards
Exebridge, Dulverton TA22 9AZ

Tel 01398 324453
Web www.staghound.co.uk

Sannacott

On the southern fringes of Exmoor you're in huntin' and shootin' country. This is a stud farm – the Trickeys breed national hunt racehorses – and there's a riding stables close by. Downstairs is a happy mix of casual countryside living, antiques, open fires and family pictures. Bedrooms are traditional, clean and comfortable, all have lovely long views across rolling hills and trees, and you can come and go as you please. Clare bakes her own bread, most produce is organic or local and there's a pretty cottagey garden to wander through. Great for walkers, riders, birdwatchers and nature lovers.

Price	£60-£70.
Rooms	3: 1 double; 1 twin/double sharing bath. Annexe: 1 twin with separate bath/shower.
Meals	Occasional dinner, 3 courses, £20. Pub 5 miles.
Closed	Rarely.
Directions	M5 J27; A361 for Barnstaple, past Tiverton, 15.5 miles; right at r'bout (small sign Whitechapel). 1.5 miles to junc., right towards Twitchen & N. Molton; 1.5m to 3rd on left, black gates.

Mrs E C Trickey
North Molton EX36 3JS

Tel 01598 740203
Web www.sannacott.co.uk

Heasley House

A Georgian dower house in a sleepy hamlet on the southern fringes of Exmoor. Enjoy stripped floors, open fires, an eclectic collection of art and Paul's cooking: all is locally sourced; beef from Exmoor, game from nearby estates, herbs from the kitchen garden. Super comfy rooms have big beds, Egyptian cotton sheets, extra-wide baths or power showers. Breakfasts are generous, so dig in then set off for a beach day at Croyde or some great walking on Exmoor.. There are gardens back and front, the sound of running water, and Paul's collection of brandy or armagnac is not to be missed.

Price	From £120. Suite £140. Singles £90.
Rooms	8: 7 twins/doubles, 1 suite.
Meals	Dinner, 3 courses, £21.50.
Closed	Christmas Day, Boxing Day & February.
Directions	From junc. 27 M5, A361 to Barnstaple. Right at sign for North Molton, then left for Heasley Mill.

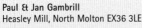

Paul & Jan Gambrill
Heasley Mill, North Molton EX36 3LE

Tel 01598 740213
Web www.heasley-house.co.uk

Sea View Villa

The sea-captain's house gazes down from its wooded perch on beautiful Lynmouth below. There's a short, steep path up… then the pampering begins. Chris cooks, Steve does (sparkling) front of house. Bedrooms are warm and vibrant in black and silver, ochre and cream, and dinner is a full blown performance with theatrical touches: perfumed candles, soft music, maybe local lamb then "flambé Jamaican bananas". Rise early for a glorious Exmoor safari (spot the red deer) then ease away your aches and pains with an in-house holistic massage. The attention to detail here is fabulous.

Price	£90-£110. Singles £40.
Rooms	4: 2 doubles; 2 twins sharing bath.
Meals	Dinner, 5 courses, £30.
Closed	January-mid-February.
Directions	From M5 exit 23; A39 for Minehead; on to Porlock along coast to Lynmouth. Sea View Villa off Watersmeet Road, up path, directly opp. church.

Steve Williams & Chris Bissex
6 Summerhouse Path, Lynmouth EX35 6ES

Tel 01598 753460
Web www.seaviewvilla.co.uk

St Vincent House & Restaurant

Jean-Paul and Lin do their own thing brilliantly; boundless kindness and fabulous food are the hallmarks. Find stripped floors, warm rugs, gilt mirrors and polished brass in front of an open fire. Spotless bedrooms have good beds, warm colours and super little bathrooms. Aperitifs are served in the front garden in summer; hop back into the restaurant for scallops cooked in butter and lemon, filet mignon with roasted garlic, lavender and vodka ice cream. John-Paul is Belgian, so are his beers, chocolate and waffles; the latter are served at breakfast with free-range eggs and local sausages.

Price	£70-£75.
Rooms	5 twins/doubles.
Meals	Dinner £24-£27.
Closed	November-Easter.
Directions	In Lynton, ignore 1st sign to left; follow signs for car parks. Up hill, see car park on left, thatched house on right; on left after car park, next to Exmoor Museum.

Jean-Paul Salpetier & Lin Cameron
Market Street, Castle Hill, Lynton EX35 6JA

Tel 01598 752244
Web www.st-vincent-hotel.co.uk

The Old Rectory

This lovely hotel stands next to an 11th-century church in three acres of mature garden: birdsong, waterfalls, scented azaleas and wild gunnera make it a wonderful spot for afternoon tea. Inside, warm interiors are restful and stylish: an open fire in the sitting room, a 200-year-old vine shading the conservatory and a big airy dining room for Stewart's delicious cooking; homemade bread, Exmoor lamb, West country cheeses – water is from a local spring. Airy bedrooms come in fresh colours with trim carpets, pressed white linen, garden flowers and bowls of fruit that include grapes from the vine in season. *Minimum stay two nights at weekends.*

Price	Half-board (breakfast, dinner, afternoon tea) £97.50-£127.50 p.p.
Rooms	8: 2 doubles, 6 twins/doubles.
Meals	Half-board only. Dinner for non-residents, £35.
Closed	November-February.
Directions	M5 junc. 27, A361 to South Molton, then A399 north. Right at Blackmore Gate onto A39 for Lynton. Left after 3 miles, signed Martinhoe, just past Woody Bay Station. In village, next to church.

Stewart Willis & Chris Legg
Martinhoe, Exmoor National Park, EX31 4QT

Tel 01598 763368
Web www.oldrectoryhotel.co.uk

Southcliffe Hall

An Argentinian chandelier, antique French radiators, a rediscovered Victorian garden; we love this gorgeous, grandly idiosyncratic house overlooking the sea. Eccentric owners have left their mark on what was originally the Manor House. Kate and Barry are young and enthusiastic. Vast bedrooms have rich carpets, big beds, antique flourishes. Bathrooms are fabulous one-offs – roll top baths to porcelain loos. Tea in the drawing room or the terraces, dinner in the panelled dining room; at breakfast, local produce. Spot deer in the woodland, walk to the beach, hike along the coast. Great fun.

Price	£100. Singles by arrangement.
Rooms	1 double, 1 twin.
Meals	Dinner, 3 courses, £25. Pub 5-minute walk.
Closed	Rarely.
Directions	From A361, B3343 towards Woolacombe. Turn right, thro' Lincombe, into Lee. Long drive to house is on left, between village hall and Fuschia Tearoom.

Kate Seekings & Barry Jenkinson
Lee EX34 8LW

Tel 01271 867068
Web www.southcliffehall.co.uk

Victoria House

Beachcombers, surfers and walkers will be in their element in this Edwardian seaside villa where all of the bedrooms have magnificent views. Choose between two in the main house with state-of-the-art bathrooms and one in the annexe with a beach-hut feel and a private deck. Heather is lively and fun, she and David are ex-RAF and clearly enjoy looking after you; breakfast is a main meal of nuts, fresh fruits, yogurts, eggs benedict, smoked salmon or The Full Monty. You are on the coastal road to Woolacombe for International Surf and Kite Surfing competitions; Lundy is always in view. Bucket and spade bliss.

Price	£70-£120.
Rooms	3: 2 doubles, 1 family room.
Meals	Occasional dinner. Packed lunch £8. Pubs 200 yds.
Closed	Never.
Directions	From B3343, right for Mortehoe. Through village & past the old chapel. Down steep hill, with the bay ahead; house 3rd on left.

Heather & David Burke
Chapel Hill, Mortehoe, Woolacombe EX34 7DZ

Tel 01271 871302
Web www.victoriahousebandb.co.uk

Beachborough Country House

A gracious 18th-century rectory with stone-flagged floors, lofty windows, wooden shutters, charming gardens. Viviane is vivacious and she spoils you with seemingly effortless food straight from the Aga, either in the kitchen or in the elegant dining room with twinkling fire. Chickens cluck, horses whinny but otherwise the peace is deep; this is perfect walking or cycling country. Ease any aches and pains in a steaming roll top; bathrooms are awash with fluffy towels, large bedrooms are fresh as a daisy with great views – admire them from the window seats. Combe Martin is a short hop for a grand beach day.

Price	From £60. Singles £40.
Rooms	3: 1 twin/double, 2 doubles.
Meals	Dinner, 2-3 courses, from £16.
Closed	Rarely.
Directions	From A361 take A399 for 12 miles. At Blackmoor Gate, left onto A39. House 1.5 miles on right.

Viviane Clout
Kentisbury, Barnstaple EX31 4NH
Tel 01271 882487
Web www.beachboroughcountryhouse.co.uk

Bratton Mill

Absolute privacy down the long track to a thickly wooded and beautifully secluded valley: watch for dragonflies, red deer, buzzards and the flash of the kingfisher. To the backdrop of a rushing stream is the house, painted traditional white and filled with treasure – including Marilyn who spoils you with elegant china, fresh flowers, warm bathrooms, crisp linen and a comforting decanter of port. Breakfast is locally sourced and superb; in summer, eat by the stream to almost deafening birdsong. There are simple strolls or robust hikes straight from the door. Wonderful. *Self-catering cottage & folly available.*

Price	£75-£95. Singles from £45.
Rooms	2: 1 double/twin, 1 four-poster. Children's rooms available.
Meals	Dinner/supper available. Pub close walking distance.
Closed	Rarely.
Directions	From Bratton Fleming High Street turn into Mill Lane. Down road for 0.5 miles thro' railway cutting; turn right.

Marilyn Holloway
Bratton Fleming, Barnstaple EX31 4RU

Tel 01598 710026
Web www.brattonmill.co.uk

Hewish Barton

The second you arrive you're 'away from it all'. In the majestic Georgian house framed by green hills and a garden bouncing with birds, Maggi gives you delicious homemade cake for tea. You get a kitchen, too, and a lovely log-fired sitting room full of artefacts and books. Bedrooms have big sash windows, generous wardrobes and amazing views; baths encourage long soaks. Come for home comforts, home cooking, breakfasts by the Aga, woodland paths… and Woolacombe and Ilfracombe (the next Padstow?) down the road. Good value, great for couples *and* house parties, and the loveliest hosts.

Price	From £70. Singles from £37.50.
Rooms	3 doubles. Guest kitchen.
Meals	Dinner, 3 courses, from £20 (min. 6). BYO. Pub 2 miles.
Closed	Rarely.
Directions	A361 to Barnstaple. Follow A39 past hospital, left onto B3230 to Ilfracombe. Thro' Muddiford; 1 mile, quarry on left, right into drive.

Maggi & Keith Wase
Muddiford, Barnstaple EX31 4HH

Tel 01271 850245
Web www.hewish-barton.co.uk

Broomhill Art Hotel & Sculpture Gardens

Broomhill is a one off and anyone with the slightest interest in art will love it here. You find original pieces on every wall, and a dazzling sculpture garden that's floodlit at night; huge bronzes lurk behind trees, paths cut through ten acres of glorious woodland. Step inside and find galleries all around (no guest sitting room, just sofas in the galleries). Simple bedrooms, now refurbished, are good value for money – all have pretty linen and original art. Slow food has a Mediterranean touch and mixes organic produce, local seafood, fair trade goods and fresh vegetables from neighbouring farms. *Minimum stay two nights, half-board at weekends.*

Price	£70. Singles from £45. Weekends (Fri & Sat) half-board only, £205 per room.
Rooms	6: 4 doubles, 2 twins.
Meals	Lunch from £5 (Wed-Sun). Dinner Fri & Sat only.
Closed	20 December-mid-January.
Directions	From Barnstaple, A39 north towards Lynton, then left onto B3230 for Ilfracombe. On left 2 miles after NDD Hospital.

Rinus & Aniet Van de Sande
Muddiford, Barnstaple EX31 4EX

Tel	01271 850262
Web	www.broomhillart.co.uk

Hillbrow House

You could be forgiven for thinking this 'house on the hill' is genuine Georgian – but it's mostly new, with a deep veranda and glorious views over the golf course (and, on a clear day, to distant Dartmoor). The light, uncluttered rooms are neat as a pin with coordinated colours, thick fabrics, antiques and your own upstairs studio sitting room; bedrooms have feather pillows, proper blankets and luxurious bathrooms. Golfers and walkers will be in paradise, surfers can reach Croyde easily and a plethora of gentler beaches lie in the other direction. Stoke up on delicious homemade granola for breakfast.

Price	From £80. Singles £45.
Rooms	2: 1 double; 1 double with separate bath.
Meals	Dinner, 3 courses, £25. Pubs/restaurants within walking distance.
Closed	Christmas.
Directions	Take B3226 from South Molton for 5 miles. Turn right for Chittlehamholt, left at T-junc, then through village. House is last on right.

Clarissa Roe
Chittlehamholt EX37 9NS

Tel 01769 540214
Web www.hillbrowhouse.com

Lower Hummacott

Bright clear colours, antique furniture, charming decorative touches. There are fresh fruit and flowers in the bedrooms (one with a king-size bed) and two guest sitting rooms. Delicious, organic and traditionally reared meat, veg and eggs, fresh fish, homemade cakes. As if that were not enough, the Georgian farmhouse has a stunning formal garden created from scratch – spring-fed pools, lime walk, pergola, arches, herbaceous beds and a new gazebo. Liz, a weaver, and Tony, an award-winning artist (he has a gallery in the house) are charming and friendly and look after you beautifully.

Price	£66.
Rooms	2 doubles.
Meals	Dinner £27 (Sunday & Monday only). Pub/restaurant 1.5 miles.
Closed	Rarely.
Directions	0.5 miles east of Kings Nympton village is Beara Cross; go straight over marked to Romansleigh for 0.75 miles; Hummacott is 1st entrance on left by the iron wheel.

Tony & Liz Williams
Kings Nympton, Umberleigh EX37 9TU
Tel 01769 581177

Northcote Manor

Fabulous countryside, beautiful gardens, an ancient and elegant tall-chimneyed house. Cheryl will quietly and professionally show you through the studded oak doors to large, light, comfortable rooms with big windows, cosy chairs, fires in winter. The colours are creams, yellows and blues; some chintzes mixed with stripes and tapestries on deep window seats. Old-fashioned bedrooms with dark antique furniture are a good size, all have lovely views, fresh flowers in tall vases and warm, spotless bathrooms. Eat well in the formal dining room with its hand-painted wall murals.

Price	£155-£250. Singles from £90. Half-board (min. 2 nights) from £100 p.p.
Rooms	11: 4 doubles, 2 twins/doubles, 1 four-poster, 4 suites.
Meals	Dinner £38.
Closed	Rarely.
Directions	M5 junc. 27, A361 to S. Molton. Fork left onto B3227; left on A377 for Exeter. Entrance 4.1 miles on right, signed.

Cheryl King
Burrington, Umberleigh EX37 9LZ

Tel 01769 560501
Web www.northcotemanor.co.uk

Horry Mill

A former miller's cottage in rural bliss. The beamed sitting room has a plentiful supply of logs, there are wide oak stairs, gleaming floor boards in the bedrooms, lots of games and books, and nice china. Milk and newspapers can be delivered, and, when Sonia's not looking after their Aberdeen Angus cattle, she will shop for you, so you can put the car in mothballs. She and Simon, who live a little way away, are homely and welcoming. You'll love Simon's pièce de résistance: a beautiful, wooden thatched summer house a step from your door. Peaceful and untouched: a perfect place for star-gazing.

Price	£300-£580 per week.
Rooms	Cottage for 4 (1 double, 1 twin; bath & shower room).
Meals	Restaurants/pubs within 1-hour walk.
Closed	Never.
Directions	Directions given on booking.

Simon & Sonia Hodgson
Hollocombe, Chulmleigh EX18 7QH
Tel 01769 520266
Web www.horrymill.com

Beara Farmhouse

The moment you arrive at the whitewashed farmhouse you feel the affection your hosts have for the place. Richard is a lover of wood and a fine craftsman – every room echoes his talent; he also created the pond that's home to mallards and geese. Ann has laid brick paths, stencilled, stitched and painted, all with an eye for colour; bedrooms and guest sitting room are delectable and snug. Open farmland all around, sheep, pigs and hens in the yard, the Tarka Trail on your doorstep and hosts happy to give you 6.30am breakfast should you plan a day on Lundy Island. Readers love this place. *Minimum two nights June-Sept.*

Price	£65. Singles by arrangement.
Rooms	2: 1 double, 1 twin.
Meals	Pub 1.5 miles.
Closed	20 December-5 January.
Directions	From A39, left into Bideford, round quay, past old bridge on left. Signs to Torrington; 1.5 miles, right for Buckland Brewer; 2.5 miles, left; 0.5 miles, right over cattle grid & down track.

Ann & Richard Dorsett
Buckland Brewer, Bideford EX39 5EH

Tel 01237 451666
Web www.bearafarmhouse.co.uk

The Stables

Biscuits, flowers and a glowing log-burner on arrival, breakfast whenever you want it, wellies and waxed jackets on tap. Rupert and Kim are busy farmers and artist/designers (ask to see their beautiful garden trugs) who choose to give guests what they would most like themselves. So... you have the whole of the stables to yourselves, tranquil, beautifully restored and with field and sky views. Downstairs is open-plan plus kitchen; upstairs, sloping ceilings, warm wood floors, big bed, soft towels. It's cosy yet spacious, stylish yet homely, and the Atlantic coast is the shortest drive.

Price	£75. Singles £50.
Rooms	Barn for 2: 1 double, sitting room & kitchen.
Meals	Pub 3 miles.
Closed	Never.
Directions	A39 to Woolfardisworthy. At T-junc. in village, left. 0.5 miles left to Stibb X. Over bridge bear right, then left. Uphill, right towards Leworthy & Mill; 0.5 miles; on left.

Rupert & Kim Ashmore
Leworthy Barton, Woolsery, Bideford EX39 5PY
Tel 01237 431140
Email kim@westcountrylife.co.uk

Blagdon Manor

You'll have the warmest of welcomes from Steve and Liz. There are doors that open onto the garden in the stone-flagged library, an open fire in the sitting room, a panelled bar in what was the 16th-century kitchen, and a conservatory for breakfast where you can watch the birds flit by. Bedrooms have decanters of sherry and fresh flowers, warm country florals and bathrobes. Colours are bold: blues, yellows, lilacs and greens; one room has a fine purple carpet. You get small sofas if there's room, the odd beam, a bit of chintz and comfortably snug bathrooms. Steve's cooking is not to be missed.

Price	£125. Singles £85.
Rooms	7: 5 doubles, 2 twins/doubles.
Meals	Lunch from £17 (Wed-Sun). Dinner from £31.
Closed	2 weeks in January; 2 weeks in October; New Year.
Directions	A30, then north from Launceston on A388. Ignore signs to Ashwater. Right at Blagdon Cross, signed. Right; right again; house signed right.

Steve & Liz Morey
Ashwater EX21 5DF

Tel 01409 211224
Web www.blagdon.com

Shifting Sands

Rome wasn't built in a day – but Shifting Sands was – two hours in fact was all it took for its youthful architects, clad only in shorts and sun hats, to fashion it using local materials. The diminuitive owner, Leilani, has a tragic history having been whisked off by a freak wave while doing the hula hula, only to end up here – she never stops smiling though. Copious bedrooms are slightly cramped – actually it's quite tricky to get into them at all. Go for the sea view rooms from where you can watch the incoming tide – like a hawk! A thoroughly fleeting place to stay, with – some would say – the ideal, silent hostess.

Price	Bucketloads.
Rooms	A bit crumbly usually.
Meals	Sandwiches only.
Closed	Nightly for rebuilding works.
Directions	You can't miss it unless it's not there.

Miss Leilani Lonely
The Beach, Hope Shingle
Tel Not connected.
Email hulahula@sawdays.co.uk

The Arundell Arms

A tiny interest in fishing would not go amiss. Anne, or Mrs VB as staff fondly call her, has been at the helm here for 45 years; her MBE for services to tourism is richly deserved. Over the years the hotel has resuscitated buildings at the heart of the village: the old police station and magistrates court is a pub, the old school a conference centre. The funnel-roofed old cock-fighting pit, one of only two left in England, is now the rod room. All is refurbished and tiptop, there are 20 miles of the Tamar to try your luck in, or simply search for otter and kingfishers along its bank.

Price	£160-£190. Singles from £99.
Rooms	21: 9 doubles, 7 twins, 3 singles, 2 suites.
Meals	Bar meals £7-£15. Dinner from £38.
Closed	Christmas.
Directions	A30 south-west from Exeter, past Okehampton. Lifton 0.5 miles off A30, 3 miles east of Launceston & signed. Hotel in centre of village.

Anne Voss-Bark
Lifton PL16 0AA

Tel 01566 784666
Web www.arundellarms.com

Cornwall

Photo: istock.com

The Old Vicarage

The first sight of quirky chimneys – the spires of former owner Reverend Hawker's parish churches – sets the scene for a house of theatricality. Jill, Richard and their home burst with knowledge on the eccentric vicar, local history and Victoriana. Rooms are casually grand, dotted with *objets* – brass gramophone, magic lantern, policemen's helmets. Browse books in the study, play the drawing room grand piano, sip brandy over billiards. Bedrooms are country-house pretty, bathrooms clean if cheerfully dated. Views reach to the sea. Walk off breakfast along the cliffs. Mobiles don't work. Bliss.

Price	£80. Singles £40.
Rooms	3: 1 double, 1 twin, 1 single.
Meals	Occasional dinner. Pub 10-minute walk.
Closed	December-January.
Directions	From A39 at Morwenstow, follow signs towards church. Small turning on right, just before church, marked 'public footpath'. Drive down to house.

Jill & Richard Wellby
Morwenstow EX23 9SR

Tel 01288 331369
Web www.rshawker.co.uk

Beachmodern No. 28

Inside the huge, light, Victorian villa, white walls and sanded boards create a perfect backdrop for modern art, clean lines, a gizmo-packed living room with leather sofas and a log fire. The huge kitchen-dining room is brilliant for large parties and comfy bedrooms are scattered with cushions and throws; paintings and furniture add splashes of colour and you can glimpse the sea from most. There's a barbecue in the garden; the beach, which stretches for three miles at low tide, is a five minute walk. Bude's restaurants and bars, its surfing beaches and the coastal path are two minutes away.

Price	£1,320-£5,000 per week.
Rooms	House for 2-20 (3 doubles, 1 double with single, 3 twins/triples, 1 single/twin; 3 bathrooms).
Meals	Bude 2-minute walk. Private chef can be provided.
Closed	Never.
Directions	Directions given on booking.

Emma Flanagan
28 Downs View, Bude EX23 8RG

Tel 01288 275006
Web www.beachmodern.com

Crooklets House & Crooklets View

A five-minute walk from Bude, this is seaside living at its most luxurious: contemporary kitchens in farmhouse style, new leather sofas, roll top baths on Italian marble or walnut floors, cream linen drapes, wrought-iron beds, sumptuous linen, elaborate tiled floors and fireplaces, and white sash windows and cornices. Two tremendous sand and surf beaches are nearby but the buckets you'll be using here are as likely to be for champagne and ice. Light floods in and the views are wonderful; from a teak-furnished patio you may watch the kids on the beach. *Houses interconnect for one party. Chef optional.*

Price	£750-£3,250 per week.
Rooms	Crooklets House for 12. Crooklets View for 14.
Meals	Bude 5-minute walk; pub up the road.
Closed	Never.
Directions	Directions given on booking.

Nick Compton
Crooklets, Bude EX23 8NE
Tel 01288 355755
Email nick@breakwater-holidays.co.uk

Upton Farm

A restored farmhouse set back from the rugged coastline with unrivalled views, from Tintagel to Port Isaac and beyond... sunsets are sublime. Bedrooms are traditional and smart, there's a games room and safe storage for surfers. Slate slabs in the hall, gentle colours throughout; from the depths of the sea-green sofa in your drawing room, breathe in those AONB views. Such seclusion! Yet ten minutes across fields is the coastal path and, nearby, serious surfing, great pub, restaurant and more. Kick-start your day with Ricardo's signature muesli. *Minimum stay two nights July & Aug. Children over eight welcome.*

Price	£85-£95. Singles from £60.
Rooms	3: 2 doubles, 1 twin.
Meals	Pub/restaurant 1 mile.
Closed	Rarely.
Directions	South through Delabole, near end of village right into Treligga Downs Rd; 0.5 miles to T-junc; turn right. 1 mile on, pass Trecarne Farm on left; 100 yds, house on right.

Elizabeth & Ricardo Dorich
Trebarwith PL33 9DG

Tel 01840 770225
Web www.upton-farm.co.uk

Upton Farm Barn & Mill

Scrunch up a swathe of white granite driveway and enter an enclosed courtyard garden (both Mill and Barn have one) dotted with young shrubs. Bedrooms are on the ground floor, living areas are on the first, roof beams are exposed to stunning effect and views are rural. There are big sofas and, in the Mill, a wood-burner; you get masses of space in which to sprawl, attractive coir strewn with rugs, shelves stocked with good books and games and well-planned, high-spec kitchens. The games room is shared – a godsend in bad weather – and the friendly owners do B&B next door. Fabulous.

Price	Hyde Barn £500-£1,155. Upton Mill £900-£2,200. Prices per week.
Rooms	Hyde Barn for 6. Upton Mill for 8-10.
Meals	Restaurants/pubs within 20-minute walk.
Closed	Rarely.
Directions	Directions given on booking.

Elizabeth & Ricardo Dorich
Trebarwith PL33 9DG

Tel 01840 770225
Web www.upton-farm.co.uk

Upper & Lower Tregudda

Such a lovely little bay and these two apartments, set on a small hillside, have Atlantic views to die for. Nothing particularly swish or stylish inside, but they are light, warm and comfortable; taken together they're perfect for a large family gathering. Upper Tregudda has a separate dining room and a large sitting room with huge windows overlooking all that sea and your own terrace for a sundowner; Lower Tregudda has direct access to the shared lawn area. Down the hill is a 17th-century inn, delightful Port Isaac is near and glorious rock pools will keep the kids happy for hours.

Price	£567-£1,254 per week.
Rooms	2 apartments for 8.
Meals	Restaurant/pubs in Port Isaac.
Closed	Never.
Directions	Directions given on booking.

c/o The Port Gaverne Hotel
Port Gaverne, Port Isaac PL29 3SQ

Tel 01208 880293
Web www.greendoorcottages.co.uk

Caradoc of Tregardock

Crashing breakers, wheeling gulls, carpets of wild flowers in the spring; a dream for artists and a tonic for everyone. Walk down to the secluded tidal beach with two miles of sand, rock pools, caves and some tricky surfing. The sympathetically restored listed buildings are set around a grassy courtyard within 300 acres of farmland. You can B&B or self cater – all is perfect for large or small groups and there's a studio for art and yoga. Bedrooms are light and airy with white walls and uninterrupted Atlantic views. There are large, safe lawns and a summerhouse and deck for glorious sunsets. *Cream teas.*

Price	£90-£140. Singles £45-£70. Under 5s free.
Rooms	4 twins/doubles.
Meals	Dinner £35. Pubs/restaurants 2 miles. Private chef special occasions.
Closed	Rarely.
Directions	Take turn to Treligga off B3314; 2nd farm road, signed.

Janet Cant
Treligga, Port Isaac PL33 9ED

Tel 01840 213300
Web www.tregardock.com

Caradoc & Julian's House

Escape to a delightful coastal retreat, either in the converted barn or the cottage farmhouse: you are a long way from anyone else and a field and a half from a secret sandy cove – perfect for rock pools at low tide. Arrive to a Cornish cream tea and immediately feel at home; crackling log fires in winter, comfy sofas, books, music and videos, plenty of space and a traditional farmhouse kitchen. Outside there are large safe gardens, green fields and a gorgeous summer house for watching the sun set over the sea. Take both properties at the same time for large house parties and big family get-togethers.

Price	£500-£2,000 per week.
Rooms	Julian's House for 4: 2 twins/doubles; bath/shower room. Caradoc for 8: 3 twins/doubles with bath/shower; 1 twin/double with shower.
Meals	Pubs/restaurants 2 miles. Home-cooked freezer meals available.
Closed	Never.
Directions	Take turn to Treligga off B3314; 2nd farm road, signed.

Janet Cant
Treligga, Port Isaac PL33 9ED
Tel 01840 213300
Email info@tregardock.com

Cornish Tipi Holidays

A magical, laid-back world – 37 tipis of white canvas with colourful linings. The floors are covered with Turkish rugs; there are bed-rolls, North African lanterns, a powerful camping-gaz light, a baby Belling cooker, kitchen box full of utensils, and all you need to start a camp fire outside. You walk to the lovely wooden shower blocks and loos. In fact you walk everywhere once you have arrived; no cars are allowed after unloading. The site is in 16 acres of undulating woodland, streams and grass pathways meander through and there is a long, beautiful lake where you can swim and catch fish.

Price	£375-£745 per week. Short breaks £275-£425.
Rooms	37 tipis, 1 yurt: for max. 3, max. 6 & max. 12; 3 shower blocks.
Meals	Self-catering.
Closed	November-March.
Directions	From A395, follow B3314 to and through Delabole; left at Port Gaverne x-road, 1.5 miles.

Ms Elizabeth Tom
c/o Tregeare, Pendoggett, St Kew PL30 3HZ
Tel 01208 880781
Web www.cornish-tipi-holidays.co.uk

Tremoren

Views stretch sleepily over the Cornish countryside. You might feel inclined to do nothing more than snooze over your book on the terrace, but the surfing beaches, the Camel Trail and the Eden Project are all close by. The stone and slate former farmhouse has been smartly updated with a light and airy ground-floor bedroom – all soft colours, pretty china and crisp bed linen – and a swish, power-shower bathroom. Your red-walled sitting room, full of books and interesting maps, leads out onto the flower-filled terrace: perfect for that evening drink. Lanie is bubbly and engaging, and food is her passion.

Price	£80.
Rooms	1 double & sitting room.
Meals	Dinner, 4 courses, £25. Inn 0.5 miles.
Closed	Rarely.
Directions	A39 to St Kew Highway through village; left at Red Lion. Down lane, 1st left round sharp right-hand bend. 2nd drive on right; signed.

Philip & Lanie Calvert
St Kew, Bodmin PL30 3HA

Tel 01208 841790
Web www.sunsell.com/clients/tremoren

Polrode Mill Cottage

A lovely, solid, beamy, 17th-century cottage in a birdsung valley. Inside, flagged floors, Chesterfields, a wood-burner and a light open feel. Your friendly young hosts live next door; they are working hard on the informal flower and vegetable garden, much of the produce is used in David's delicious homemade dinners, there's pumpkin marmalade and eggs from the hens. Bedrooms are cottage-cosy with stripped floors, comfy wrought-iron beds and silver cast-iron radiators; fresh bathrooms have double-ended roll top baths. A slight hum of traffic outside but no matter, inside it is blissfully peaceful.

Price	£75-£90. Singles £55.
Rooms	3 doubles.
Meals	Dinner, 3 courses, £27.
Closed	Rarely.
Directions	From A395 take A39 towards Camelford. Through Camelford; continue on A39 to Knightsmill. From there, 1.8 miles up on left-hand side.

Deborah Hilborne & David Edwards
Allen Valley, St Tudy, Bodmin PL30 3NS

Tel 01208 850203
Web www.polrodemillcottage.co.uk

Higher Lank Farm

Families rejoice: you can only come if you have a child under five! Celtic crosses in the garden and original panelling hint at the house's 500-year history; one bedroom is resplendent with oak, the other two more traditional. Nursery teas begin at 5pm, grown-up suppers are later and Lucy will cheerfully babysit while the rest of you slink off to the pub. Farm-themed playgrounds are covered in safety matting and grass, there are piglets and chicks, a pony to ride, eggs to collect, a nursery rhyme trail, a sand barn for little ones and cream teas in the garden. Oh, and real nappies are provided!

Price	From £85. Singles by arrangement.
Rooms	3 family rooms.
Meals	Supper £16.25. Nursery tea £4.75. Packed lunch £7. Pub 1.5 miles.
Closed	November-Easter.
Directions	From Launceston, A395, then A39 thro' Camelford. Left onto B3266 to Bodmin. After 4 miles, left signed Wenfordbridge Pottery; over bridge, past pottery & on brow of hill, left into lane; house at top.

Lucy Finnemore
St Breward, Bodmin PL30 4NB

Tel 01208 850716
Web www.higherlankfarm.co.uk

Lavethan

A glorious house in the most glorious of settings: views sail down to the valley. It rambles on many levels and is part 15th-century: walls are stone, floors are flagged, stairs are oak. The bedrooms in the house are lovely; one, part of the old chapel, has stone lintels that cross it, all are sunny, with proper bathrooms and lovely old baths for wallowing in. Catherine is a warm hostess and has decorated lavishly in country style; the guest sitting room is hugely welcoming with books, flowers and piano. All this and acres of ancient woods, Celtic crosses and a heated pool in the old walled garden. *Children over ten welcome.*

Price	£70-£90. Singles £40-£50.
Rooms	4: 2 twins/doubles; 2 doubles, each with separate bath.
Meals	Occasional dinner £25. Pub 0.25 miles.
Closed	Rarely.
Directions	From A30, turn for Blisland. There, past church on left & pub on right. Take lane at bottom left of village green. 0.25 miles on, drive on left (granite pillars & cattle grid).

Christopher & Catherine Hartley
Blisland, Bodmin PL30 4QG

Tel 01208 850487
Web www.lavethan.com

Cabilla Manor

Rich, exotic rugs, cushions and artefacts from around the world, and Louella's sumptuous hand-stencilled fabrics and furniture. There's a treasure round every corner of this fine manor on the edge of Bodmin Moor, and an opera house in one of the barns. Huge beds, coir carpets and garden flowers in your rooms, a dining room crammed floor to ceiling with books, many of them Robin's (a writer and explorer). A lofty conservatory for meals overlooks elegant lawns, garden and tennis court; the views are heavenly, the hosts wonderful and the final mile thrillingly wild.

Price	£80. Singles £40.
Rooms	4: 1 double; 2 doubles, 1 twin, sharing 2 baths.
Meals	Dinner, 3 courses, £30. Pub 4 miles. Restaurant 8-10 miles.
Closed	Christmas & New Year.
Directions	6 miles after Jamaica Inn on A30, left for Cardinham. Through Millpool & straight on, ignoring further signs to Cardinham. After 2.5 miles, left to Manor 0.75 miles; on right down drive.

Robin & Louella Hanbury-Tenison
Mount, Bodmin PL30 4DW

Tel 01208 821224
Web www.cabilla.co.uk

Roskear

Rosina modestly refers to her home as offering "simple cottage B&B" but this is just perfect as a rural retreat and for families, with all the attractions ten minutes by car. A large sitting room with log fire, a warm and smiling hostess, estuary views, happy dogs, clucking hens – this is countryside at its most charming. There's a sunny spot in the garden for summer breakfasts served on blue china, 30 acres of woodland and 40 of grassland to explore – and dining in one of the famous restaurants in Padstow. The Camel cycle trail is nearby and you can hire bikes locally. Uncomplicated, good value.

Price	From £60. Singles £30.
Rooms	2: 1 double with separate bath; 1 double sharing bath (let to same party only).
Meals	Pubs/restaurants 0.5-6 miles.
Closed	Rarely.
Directions	Bypass Wadebridge on A39 for Redruth. Over bridge, pass Esso garage on left; then first right to Edmonton. By modern houses turn immed. right to Roskear over cattle grid.

Rosina Messer-Bennetts
St Breock, Wadebridge PL27 7HU

Tel 01208 812805
Web www.roskear.com

Porteath Barn

What a spot! This upside-down house is elegantly uncluttered and cool with seagrass flooring and a wood-burner in the sitting room. Bedrooms – not vast – have fresh flowers, quilted bedspreads and there's an Italian marble shower room; the feel is private with your own doors to the lovely, large garden. Walks from here down a path with ponds will take you to Epphaven Cove and the beach at the bottom of the valley or to a good pub for supper if you're feeling hearty. The Bloors have perfected the art of B&B-ing, being kind and helpful without being intrusive. *Children over 12 or by arrangement.*

Price	From £75. Singles by arrangement.
Rooms	3: 2 twins/doubles, each with separate bath or shower; 1 double let to same party only.
Meals	Pub 1.5 miles.
Closed	Rarely.
Directions	A39 to Wadebridge. At r'bout follow signs to Polzeath, then to Porteath Bee Centre. Through Bee Centre shop car park, down farm track; house signed on right after 150 yds.

Jo & Michael Bloor
St Minver, Wadebridge PL27 6RA
Tel 01208 863605
Email mbloor@ukonline.co.uk

Molesworth Manor

The house – big enough to swallow hoards of people – is filled with art and interesting antiques, cool pastel colours and restored architectural features. A carved staircase leads to bedrooms that vary in style and size: two at the front are grand, those in the eaves are bright and beamed. The rectory garden is mature, well-tended and peaceful, with a small play area for children. The delicious whiff of homemade muffins will lure you down to breakfast in the gorgeous tropical-style conservatory. Beaches, coastal paths and great cycling are all there for heartier souls.

Price	£54-£100. Cottage £485-£820 per week. Whole house available.
Rooms	9 + 1: 7 doubles, 1 twin/double; 1 twin with separate shower. Self-catering cottage for 6.
Meals	Restaurants in Padstow.
Closed	November-January. Open off-season by arrangement for larger parties.
Directions	Off A389 between Wadebridge & Padstow. 300 yards from bridge in Little Petherick.

Geoff French & Jessica Clarke
Little Petherick, Padstow PL27 7QT
Tel 01841 540292
Web www.molesworthmanor.co.uk

Ballaminers House

Slate slabs, planked floors and deep sash windows with field views in this welcoming old farmhouse five minutes from Padstow. Generous, artistic Amanda serves delicious breakfasts in a heritage green room elegant with family heirlooms and small chandelier – or outdoors in summer. The cosy, light bedrooms are spotless and charming, with Designers Guild fabrics, soft colours, Balinese touches. Thoughtful extras include magazines, fruit basket, bath oils and Indonesian dressing gowns; one bathroom has a roll top tub that fits two! In the garden a series of hedged 'rooms' provide flowers for the house. *Children over ten welcome.*

Price	£70-£85. Singles £55-£85.
Rooms	3: 2 doubles, 1 twin, sharing 2 bathrooms.
Meals	Pubs/restaurants 5-minute drive.
Closed	Never.
Directions	A39 after Wadebridge, signed A389 Padstow. Reach Little Petherick; over hump bridge to whitewashed cottage at corner of unmarked lane; left up lane bearing right; on right, opp. pink house.

Amanda Fearon
Little Petherick, Padstow PL27 7QT
Tel 01841 540933
Web www.ballaminershouse.co.uk

Mother Ivey Cottage

So close to the sea that there are salt splashes on the windows! Exceptionally lovely hosts here and a simple refuge from crashing surf and Atlantic winds. Look out of the window to the big blue below, swim to the lifeboat launch, barbecue on the beach. The coastal path is stunning and you can walk to surfing beaches or just drop down to the quiet bay beneath your window. Cultured, kind hosts and a relaxed atmosphere, but bedrooms and bathrooms are basic so not for those who like their B&Bs stylish or sparkling. Families love it.

Price	From £60. Singles by arrangement.
Rooms	2 twins. Extra single bed.
Meals	Dinner from £20. Packed lunch from £5.
Closed	Rarely.
Directions	From St Merryn, right for Trevose Head. Over sleeping policemen. After tollgate ticket machine, right thro' 2nd farm gate. On towards sea; cottage gate at end of track, on right.

Phyllida & Antony Woosnam-Mills
Trevose Head, Padstow PL28 8SL
Tel 01841 520329
Email antony@trevosehead.co.uk

Calize Country House

Beneath wheeling gulls and close to blond beaches, the big square 1870 house has amazing views of skies and sea. Virginia Woolf's lighthouse is in the bay and winter seals cavort at the colony nearby. A fresh, uncomplicated décor brings the tang of the sea to every room. Art works recall a world of surf; deckchair stripes clothe the dining table and dress the window; traditional sofas call for quiet times with a book. Upstairs, patterned or pale walls, practical bath or shower rooms, perhaps a sea view. Jilly and Nigel are testament to the benefits of sea air and look after you beautifully.

Price	£80-£90. Singles £50.
Rooms	4: 2 doubles, 1 twin, 1 single.
Meals	Packed lunch £5. Pub 350 yds.
Closed	Rarely.
Directions	Exit A30 at Camborne (West) A3047. Left, then right at r'bout. Right on entering Conner Downs, then on for 2 miles. House on right after sign for Gwithian.

Jilly Whitaker
Gwithian, Hayle TR27 5BW

Tel 01736 753268
Web www.calize.co.uk

Treglisson

This is minutes from St Ives, the glorious bay and some nifty surfing beaches. Inside the old farmhouse, all is calm and peaceful. Stephen and Heather are thoughtful, fun, easy-going and filled with enthusiasm for looking after you: large light bedrooms in soft colours, generous beds with lovely linen, modern white bathrooms, good art on the walls, a beautiful antique-marble hall floor. Cornish Aga-cooked breakfasts can be relished late if you prefer; in the evening, take a sundowner to the pretty conservatory or curl up with a book in the guest sitting room. There's a heated indoor pool too. Great value.

Price	£50-£70. Singles from £30.
Rooms	4: 1 double, 1 twin, 2 family rooms.
Meals	Pubs/restaurants 2-5 miles.
Closed	Christmas & New Year.
Directions	A30 to Hayle; 4th exit on r'bout into Hayle. Left at mini r'bout into Guildford Rd; up hill for 1 mile. Turn left at green sign into lane.

Stephen & Heather Reeves
Wheal Alfred Road, Hayle TR27 5JT
Tel 01736 753141
Web www.treglisson.co.uk

Drym Farm

Rural, but not too deeply: the Tate at St Ives is a 15-minute drive. The 1705 farmhouse, beautifully revived, is surrounded by ancient barns, a dairy and a forge, fascinating to Cornish historians. Jan arrived in 2002, with an enthusiasm for authenticity and simple, stylish good taste. French limestone floors in the hall, striking art on the walls, a roll top bath, a *bateau lit*, an antique brass bed. Paintwork is fresh cream and taupe. There are old fruit trees and young camellias, a TV-free sitting room with two plump sofas and organic treats at breakfast. Charming and utterly peaceful.

Price	£70-£90. Singles from £55.
Rooms	3: 2 doubles each with separate bath; 1 twin sharing bath.
Meals	Pubs/restaurants within 4 miles.
Closed	Rarely.
Directions	From A30 to Hayle; through Hayle to r'bout, left to Helston. At Leedstown, left towards Drym. Follow road until right turn to Drym. Farm fourth on lane, on right after Drym House.

Jan Bright
Drym, Praze-an-Beeble, Camborne TR14 0NU
Tel 01209 831039
Web www.drymfarm.co.uk

House at Gwinear

An island of calm – it sits, as it has for 500 years, in its own bird-trilled acres a short drive from St Ives. The mood is now artistic, for the Halls are devoted to the encouragement of the arts and crafts which is reflected in their lifestyle. There's no stuffiness – just fresh flowers on the breakfast table, a piano in the corner, rugs on polished floors and masses of books. In a separate wing you have a cosy bedroom and sitting room and a fine view of the church from the bath. The big, lawn-filled gardens are there for bare-footed solace, and your interesting hosts couldn't be nicer.

Price	From £65.
Rooms	1 twin/double & sitting room.
Meals	Occasional dinner. Pub 1.5 miles.
Closed	Rarely.
Directions	From A30 exit Hayle (Loggans Moor r'bout); 100 yds left at mini-r'bout; 400 yds left for Gwinear; 1.5 miles, top of hill, driveway on right, just before 30mph Gwinear sign.

Charles & Diana Hall
Gwinear, St Ives TR27 5JZ
Tel 01736 850444
Email charleshall@btinternet.com

The Old Vicarage

Artists will be inspired, not just with the proximity to St Ives but with Jackie's dazzling collection of her own and other artists' work. This is a light, airy, welcoming house whose big sash windows overlook a subtropical garden; wander at will after a grand breakfast of fresh fruit and local bacon and sausages. Bedrooms have soft coloured walls, deeply comfortable beds, period furniture and more lovely artwork adding spots of colour; bathrooms are gleaming and fresh. There's a sandy beach 20-minutes' walk away and you can join the coastal path just up the road. Wonderful house, lovely owner.

Price	£65-£75. Singles £35-£40.
Rooms	3: 1 twin; 1 double with separate bath, 1 single sharing bath (same party only).
Meals	Pubs 5-8 minute walk. Restaurants in St Ives 2.5 miles.
Closed	1 November-15 March.
Directions	A30 dir. Penzance. At 2nd Hayle r'bout, A3074 St Ives. After Wyvale Garden Centre, over mini r'bout; right at next one & into Lelant. Brush End is lane on left after sign for Elm Farm. House at end.

Jackie & Howard Hollingsbee
Brush End, Lelant, St Ives TR26 3EF
Tel 01736 753324
Web www.oldvicaragelelant.co.uk

Boskerris Hotel

A quietly swanky hotel with glass everywhere framing huge views of ocean and headland. Step inside for bleached boards and smart sofas in the sitting room, fresh flowers and blond wood in the dining room. Airy bedrooms are uncluttered, with silky throws, padded headboards, crisp white linen, flat-screen TVs and DVD players. Most rooms have the view, all have fancy bathrooms, some have deep baths and deluge showers. Take the coastal path to St Ives and follow the mazy streets to the Tate; spin back for delicious locally sourced food in the restaurant or stop at Porthminster Café for the fanciest nosh in town.

Price	£90-£200. Singles from £65.
Rooms	15: 12 doubles, 3 twins.
Meals	Dinner, 3 courses, about £25.
Closed	Christmas & New Year.
Directions	A30 past Hayle, then A3074 for St Ives. After 3 miles pass brown sign for Carbis Bay, then third left. Down hill, on left.

Jonathan & Marianne Bassett
Boskerris Road, Carbis Bay, St Ives TR26 2NQ

Tel 01736 795295
Web www.boskerrishotel.co.uk

Jamies

Breathe in the sweeping ocean views from this stylish 1920s villa. Airy bedrooms are hotel-smart with white bed linen, striped or checked curtains and fresh new bathrooms; all rooms have a great feeling of space and two have sitting areas. Crisp linen and silver at the dining table create an elegant mood at breakfast – enjoy a delicious fruit salad while taking in the views, or admire some of artist Felicity's inspiring work. She and Jamie are ex-hoteliers with a great sense of fun, and can tell you about all the local restaurants, galleries and coastal walks. *Children over 12 welcome.*

Price	£100. Singles £80.
Rooms	4: 3 twins/doubles, 1 suite.
Meals	Pub 5-minute walk. Restaurants 25 minute-drive.
Closed	Rarely.
Directions	A30, then A3074 for St Ives. At Carbis Bay, Marshalls estate agents & Methodist church on left. Next right down Pannier Lane; 2nd right is Wheal Whidden; 1st house on left.

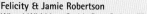

Felicity & Jamie Robertson
Wheal Whidden, Carbis Bay, St Ives TR26 2QX

Tel 01736 794718
Web www.jamiesstives.co.uk

Primrose Valley Hotel

A spade's throw from the beach, this crisp Edwardian townhouse with large windows has a cool, contemporary interior of gleaming wooden floors, modern prints and photographs, fresh flowers and uncluttered walls with bold bamboo wallpaper. Some of the bedrooms are not large but half have sea views and all have hand-stitched mattresses, fluffy towels and sleek wooden floors. Grab a paper and relax at the bar; Cornish platters of charcuterie, cheese and smoked salmon are on tap through the day and you can try something lively from the wine list served in a Riedel glass for maximum oomph. *Minimum stay two nights at weekends.*

Price	£90-£145. Suite £200-£225.
Rooms	10: 9 twins/doubles, 1 suite.
Meals	£7.50.
Closed	December & January.
Directions	From A3074 Trelyon Avenue; before hospital sign slow down, indicate right & turn down Primrose Valley; under bridge, left, then back under bridge; signs for hotel parking.

Andrew Biss
Primrose Valley, Porthminster Beach, St Ives TR26 2ED
Tel 01736 794939
Web www.primroseonline.co.uk

Organic Panda B&B & Gallery

A five-minute walk from busy St Ives, with a panoramic view of the bay: boutique B&B in perfect harmony with this artistic spot. Come for a bold scattering of modern art, a ten-seater rustic table and spacious contemporary bedrooms whose chunky beds, white walls and raw-silk cushions reveal a laid-back style. Shower rooms are small but perfectly formed. Andrea is an artist and theatre designer, Peter a photographer and organic chef; the food sounds delicious and they bake their own bread. And the most beautiful coastal road in all England leads to St Just. *Minimum stay three nights: July & August, Easter & Christmas.*

Price	£75-£120.
Rooms	3: 2 doubles, 1 twin.
Meals	Packed lunch £10. Restaurants 10-minute walk.
Closed	Rarely.
Directions	A3074 to St Ives. Signs to leisure centre; house behind 3rd sign, on left-hand bend.

Peter Williams & Andrea Carr
1 Pednolver Terrace, St Ives TR26 2EL

Tel 01736 793890
Web www.organicpanda.co.uk

Blue Hayes

No expense has been spared in the restoration of this 1922 manse with glittering views of the sea. Lights come on as if by magic, high-tech showers blast from multiple angles in state-of-the-art bathrooms and staff are great. Bedrooms have raw silk curtains, thick cotton sheets and (in four) views to the sea. A harmonious sea-blue and oatmeal palette holds court – even the cocktails are colour coordinated: enjoy yours on the large terrace as the sunset inches round the bay. Dinners are good with fresh local fish and meat presented with mouthwatering sauces; the wine list is diverse. Cossetting.

Price	£140-£190. Singles £120-£145.
Rooms	6: 4 doubles, 1 four-poster, 1 triple.
Meals	Dinner £20-£25.
Closed	December & January.
Directions	From A30 past Hayle, A3074 to St Ives through Lelant and Carbis Bay. After mini-r'bout (Tesco on left) down hill. At bottom, right immed. after garage on right.

Malcolm Herring
Trelyon Avenue, St Ives TR26 2AD
Tel 01736 797129
Web www.bluehayes.co.uk

11 Sea View Terrace

In a smart row of Edwardian villas, with views over harbour, island and sea, is a delectable retreat. Sleek, softy coloured interiors are light and gentle on the eye – an Italian circular glass table here, a painted seascape there – creating a deeply civilised feel. Bedrooms are perfect with crisp linen, vistas of whirling gulls, your own terrace; bathrooms are state-of-the-art. Rejoice in softly boiled eggs with anchovy and chive-butter soldiers for breakfast – or continental in bed if you prefer. Grahame looks after you impeccably and design aficionados will be happy. *Free admission to Tate Gallery & Barbara Hepworth Museum.*

Price	£95-£115. Singles from £70.
Rooms	3 suites.
Meals	Dinner, with wine, from £25 (groups only). Packed lunch £10. Pubs/restaurants 5-minute walk.
Closed	Rarely.
Directions	At Porthminster Hotel, signs for Tate; down Albert Rd, right just before Longships Hotel. Limited parking.

Grahame Wheelband
St Ives TR26 2DH

Tel 01736 798440
Web www.11stives.co.uk

Shutters on the Harbour

Georgina has cleverly renovated this tiny 1875 fisherman's cottage, just steps away from the beach, into a gorgeous hideaway with lots of surprising touches. From the open plan sitting room with neutral stone floor and underfloor heating, scamper into the wet room to wash off sand and dry out wet suits – perfect for surfers. Up to a mezzanine kitchen with round table, built-in benches, all mod cons and a galleried 'chill-out' space. Bedrooms have locally made beds, side tables of painted driftwood and goose down pillows. Relax into the beach-house feel and make the most of St Ives and all its delights.

Price	£500-£960 per week.
Rooms	2 doubles with shower; shower room.
Meals	Restaurants/pubs within 20-minute walk.
Closed	Never.
Directions	Directions given on booking.

Georgina Lenain
Bethesda Hill, St Ives TR26 1PB
Tel 07770 431558
Email georgitbl@hotmail.com

The Gurnard's Head

The coastline here is utterly magical and the walk up to St Ives is hard to beat. As for the hotel, you couldn't hope for a better base. It's earthy, warm, stylish and friendly, with airy interiors, colourwashed walls, stripped wooden floors and open fires in the bar. Bedrooms are warm and cosy, simple and spotless, with Vi-sprung mattresses, crisp white linen, throws over armchairs, Roberts radios. Downstairs, super food, all homemade, can be eaten wherever you want: in the bar, in the restaurant or out in the garden. Picnics are easily arranged and there's bluegrass folk music in the bar most weeks.

Price	£72.50-£125. Singles from £50.
Rooms	7: 4 doubles, 3 twins/doubles.
Meals	Lunch from £4.50. Dinner, 3 courses, about £25.
Closed	New Year.
Directions	West from St Ives on B3306. On right at head of village.

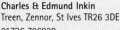

Charles & Edmund Inkin
Treen, Zennor, St Ives TR26 3DE

Tel 01736 796928
Web www.gurnardshead.co.uk

The Old Coastguard Hotel

The sea spumes over the rocks a hundred yards from your window, the hotel is easy-going and generous, the dining room airy, the meals among Cornwall's best. The produce is sourced locally, as is proper with Newlyn's fishing fleet round the corner: scallops, crab, monkfish, hake, chargrilled sirloin, honey-roast tomatoes, roasted garlic and potato purée. There is even Cornish wine. The bedrooms are simple, fresh and modern: no vast beds, no flounces, but great duvets and some of the best views in Britain. Staff are delightful, the bar is a mix of wood and steel, the village is two minutes by foot. *Minimum stay two nights at weekends in high season.*

Price	£90-£170. Singles from £45. Half-board from £75 p.p.
Rooms	21: 20 doubles, 1 single.
Meals	Lunch, 2 courses, from £18. Table d'hôte dinner £28-£35.
Closed	Christmas Day.
Directions	Follow A30 to Penzance & signs to Mousehole. Hotel on left as you enter the village. Limited parking on first come first served basis or public car park next door, £2 on departure.

Bill Treloar
The Parade, Mousehole TR19 6PR

Tel 01736 731222
Web www.oldcoastguardhotel.co.uk

The Summer House Restaurant with Rooms

A glittering find just off the harbour; Linda and Ciro run the place with energy and warmth. Food is a celebration – dishes are fresh, simple and cooked with flair; fish is bought daily from Newlyn. Outside, a walled garden of stone pots and swishing palm trees is a magical setting for candlelit dinners or alfresco breakfasts. Unwind on squashy sofas in a high-ceilinged, wooden-floored drawing room with big mirrors and art to die for; bedrooms combine chunky wooden antiques and family pieces with resourceful dabs of peppermint or lemon stripe; bathrooms are beach-house style. A happy, atmospheric place.

Price	£95-£120. Singles from £90.
Rooms	5: 4 doubles, 1 twin/double.
Meals	Dinner £29.50. Not Monday-Wednesday.
Closed	November-February.
Directions	With sea on left, along harbourside, past open-air pool, then immediate right after Queens Hotel. House 30 yds up on left. Private carpark.

Linda & Ciro Zaino
Cornwall Terrace, Penzance TR18 4HL
Tel 01736 363744
Web www.summerhouse-cornwall.com

The Abbey Hotel

The Abbey is a rare gem. The feel is of a smart country house, and the drawing room – roaring fire, huge gilt mirror, walls of books, rugs on stripped floors, arched windows that open onto the loveliest walled garden – is hard to beat. Bedrooms are grandly quirky; sink into big comfy beds wrapped up in crisp white linen and woollen blankets. There are chandeliers, quilted bedspreads, French armoires, plump-cushioned armchairs. You breakfast indulgently in a panelled dining room with a fire crackling and kind staff, who go the extra mile. The Abbey restaurant next door has a Michelin star. Exceptional.

Price	£105-£180. Suite £150-£190. Singles from £70. Flat £105-£130.
Rooms	7 + 1: 4 doubles, 1 twin, 1 family, 1 suite. Self-catering flat for 4.
Meals	Restaurants nearby.
Closed	Rarely.
Directions	Follow signs to town centre. Up hill (Market Jew St). Left at top, then fork left & 3rd on the left.

Jean & Michael Cox
Abbey Street, Penzance TR18 4AR

Tel 01736 366906
Web www.theabbeyonline.co.uk

Trezelah Farmhouse

You'll feel high here, on the moor between Penzance and St Ives. The humble manor farmhouse with solid stone walls and huge chimney breast at one end has a light and fresh interior of waxed floors, limed walls, Indian scatter rugs, books, a wood-burner and soft white sofas. Small bedrooms with fine antiques and gentle lighting will calm you, as will the unusually pretty bathrooms – and the lovely Caro who painted many of the pictures here. Stride out round the north coastal path, then take a breather at the Tinners Arms in Zennor and go all Lawrencian; this is a wonderful part of Cornwall.

Price	£70.
Rooms	3: 2 doubles; 1 twin with separate bath.
Meals	Pub 3 miles.
Closed	Rarely.
Directions	After Tesco r'bout heading into Penzance on A30, B3311 towards St Ives. Through Gulval, left at Badgers Cross towards Chysauster; left to Trezelah.

Caro Woods
Trezelah, Badgers Cross, Penzance TR20 8XD

Tel	01736 874388
Web	www.trezelah.co.uk

Ennys

Prepare to be spoiled. A fire smoulders in the sumptuous sitting room, tea is laid out in the Aga-warm kitchen, and bedrooms are luxurious: a king-size bed or an elegant modern four-poster, powerful showers and crisp white linen. The stylishness continues into the suites and everywhere there are fascinating artefacts from Gill's travels, designer fabrics and original art. The road ends at Ennys, so it is utterly peaceful; walk down to the river and along the old towpath to St Ives Bay. Or stay put: play tennis (on grass!) and swim in the heated pool sunk deep into the tropical gardens.

Price	£80-£115. Singles from £65.
Rooms	5: 2 doubles, 1 twin/double. Barn: 2 family suites.
Meals	Pub 3 miles.
Closed	8 November-20 December; 3 January-15 March.
Directions	2 miles east of Marazion on B3280, look for sign & turn left leading down Trewhella Lane between St Hilary & Relubbus. On to Ennys.

Gill Charlton
St Hilary, Penzance TR20 9BZ

Tel	01736 740262
Web	www.ennys.co.uk

Ednovean Farm

There's a terrace for each immaculate bedroom – one truly private – with views to the wild blue yonder and St Michael's Mount Bay: an enchanting outlook that changes with the passage of the day. Come for peace, space and the best of 'boutique B&B': eclectic fabrics and colours, pretty lamps, gleaming copper, fluffy bathrobes and handmade soaps. The beamed, open-plan sitting/dining area is an absorbing mix of exotic, rustic and elegant; have full breakfast here or continental in your room. A footpath through the field leads to the village; walk to glorious Prussia Cove and Cudden Point, too.

Price	£80-£90. Singles £70-£80.
Rooms	3: 2 doubles, 1 four-poster.
Meals	Pub 5-minute walk.
Closed	Christmas.
Directions	From A30 after Crowlas r'bout, A394 to Helston. 0.25 miles after next r'bout, 1st right for Perranuthnoe. Farm drive on left, signed.

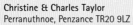

Christine & Charles Taylor
Perranuthnoe, Penzance TR20 9LZ

Tel 01736 711883
Web www.ednoveanfarm.co.uk

Hell Bay

The hotel lazes on the west coast with sublime watery views – there's nothing between you and America. Inside, you get stripped floors, coastal colours, excellent art and airy interiors. Bedrooms offer beach-house heaven, all with terraces or balconies, tongue and groove panelling, walls of windows, crisp fabrics, super bathrooms. In summer dig into crab and lobster straight from the ocean, fresh asparagus and succulent strawberries from neighbouring Tresco (don't miss its world-famous gardens). There's a sauna, a PlayStation for kids, golf for the hopeful. Low-season deals are exceptional.

Price	Half-board £130-£275 p.p. Child in parent's room £45 (incl. high tea). Under 2s free.
Rooms	25 studios & suites.
Meals	Half-board only. Lunch £5-£15.
Closed	3 January-10 February.
Directions	Ship/helicopter from Penzance, or fly to St Mary's from Bristol, Southampton, Exeter, Newquay or Land's End; boat to Bryher. Hotel can arrange.

Philip Callan
Bryher, Isles of Scilly TR23 0PR

Tel	01720 422947
Web	www.hellbay.co.uk

The Gardens

Two old miners' cottages combine to create this small, modest, well-tended home. Irish Moira, a retired midwife, adores flowers and her posies brighten every corner; Goff, a potter, tends the vegetables. Both are charming and kind. Snug bedrooms have patchwork quilts, cotton sheets, antique linen runners and plenty of books. One is on the ground floor overlooking the pretty cottage garden, two are up a narrow stair. Aga-cooked breakfasts and homemade jams are brought to the sun-streamed conservatory; in the sitting room a woodburner belts out the heat. Great value.

Price	£60-£68. Singles £30-£34.
Rooms	3: 2 doubles; 1 twin/double with separate bath.
Meals	Packed lunch from £7.50. Pubs & restaurants 10-minute drive.
Closed	Christmas & New Year.
Directions	A394 Helston to Penzance, 2nd right after Ashton Post Office for Tresowes Green. After 0.25 miles, sign for house on right.

Moira & Goff Cattell
Tresowes, Ashton, Helston TR13 9SY
Tel 01736 763299

Chydane

All that separates you from the sand and sea is the coastal path. At the far end of the spectacular, three-mile beach is Porthleven; beyond, West Penwith stretches magically into the distance. All this, and lighthouses, basking sharks, dolphins. One elegant double room, with gorgeous linen, a superb bed and a chesterfield, opens onto a French balcony overlooking the waves. The bathrooms, too, are warm and you get thick white bathrobes, lovely candles, big showers. Up steep stairs to the attic is a second room with a porthole window and a new bathroom. Walk to an excellent pub for dinner. *Children over 12 welcome.*

Price	£120. Singles £75.
Rooms	2: 1 double; 1 double with separate bathroom.
Meals	Pub/restaurant 0.5 miles.
Closed	Christmas.
Directions	From Helston A3083 to the Lizard. After 2 miles right to Gunwalloe. Right before Halzephron Inn. Chydane on right above beach.

Carla & John Caslin
Gunwalloe Fishing Cove, Helston TR12 7QB
Tel 01326 241232
Email carla.caslin@btinternet.com

Halzephron

Halzephron (cliffs of hell) has duck-your-head ceilings, stone walls, coal fires and polished brass. There are sea views from the roadside terrace, a lively courtyard for summer afternoons, and a small garden overlooking fields. Lunch on hearty homemade food then walk it off on cliff-top coastal paths. Bedrooms are country cosy, with antique dressers, quilted eiderdowns, bowls of fruit and restful florals. Both are at the back and come with long views across the fields. One has a bath, one has a shower, and there are books galore. Breakfast is cooked to order and comes with homemade marmalade.

Price	From £84. Singles £48.
Rooms	2 doubles.
Meals	Lunch & dinner: main courses £9-£17.50.
Closed	Christmas Day.
Directions	From Helston, A3083, signed The Lizard. Pass Culdrose air base, then right, signed Gunwalloe. 2 miles and inn on left after houses.

Angela Thomas
Gunwalloe, Helston TR12 7QB

Tel 01326 240406
Web www.halzephron-inn.co.uk

Halftides

Hugely enjoyable and special, surrounded by three acres with a private path down to the beach. Light-filled bedrooms are upbeat and fun with gorgeous fabrics, unusual wallpapers, crisp linen, dreamy views; bathrooms are sleek in glass and chrome. Susie is an artist and a chef and will give you a delicious organic breakfast, and a dinner of seasonal food – perhaps a barbecue in the garden in summer. Take the coastal path north or south, visit the working harbour in the village – or snaffle a packed lunch from Susie and head for the beach. This is the perfect place to relax and unwind.

Price	£75-£90. Singles £55-£60.
Rooms	3: 1 double; 1 double, 1 single sharing separate bath.
Meals	Dinner £20-£25. Packed lunch £10.
Closed	February.
Directions	A3083 to Lizard, right to Cury, 5 miles; pass Poldhu beach & enter Mullion. Right into Laflouder Lane, follow lane to very end, past sign 'Private Road'. House is 1st on right.

Charles & Susie Holdsworth Hunt
Laflouder Lane, Mullion, Helston TR12 7HU

Tel 01326 241935
Web www.halftides.co.uk

Carmelin

The setting is sensational, looking straight out to sea from the Lizard, England's most southerly point. Continental breakfasts – a feast of speciality breads, fruits, yoghurt, free-range eggs – have to fight for your attention, so spectacular are the views. The bedroom has them too – and the sun room – making a private suite with its own entrance, sitting and dining area; a gorgeous spot to sit and watch sparkling waves, white horses and sunsets. John and Jane are gentle, relaxed people who enjoy their guests; walk the coastal path and return to a lovely home-cooked meal. *French & German spoken.*

Price	From £72. Singles by arrangement.
Rooms	1 suite for 2 with separate bath/shower.
Meals	Dinner from £19. BYO. Pub within walking distance.
Closed	Rarely.
Directions	From Helston to the Lizard; at Lizard Green, right, opp. Regent Café (head for Smugglers Fish & Chips); immed. right, pass wc on left. Road unmade; on for 500 yds; double bend; 2nd on right.

Jane & John Grierson
Pentreath Lane, The Lizard TR12 7NY

Tel 01326 290677
Web www.bedandbreakfastcornwall.co.uk

Landewednack House

Susan and her pug dogs will greet you enthusiastically with tea and biscuits in the drawing room of this immaculate house. Antony the chef keeps the wheels oiled and the food coming – try his green crab soup or succulent lobster. Erik is a real gourmand and has a covetable cellar of over 2,000 bottles of wine. Bedrooms are not huge and not all have sea views, but everything you could possibly need is there, from robes to brandy. The pool area is stunning with a French feel, the garden is filled with interest and it's just a three-minute walk to the sea. *Minimum two-night stay during July & August.*

Price	From £126. Singles £63-£75.
Rooms	3: 2 doubles, 1 twin.
Meals	Dinner, 4 courses, £33-£38.
Closed	Open all year.
Directions	From Helston, A3083 south. Just before Lizard, left to Church Cove. Follow signs for about 0.75 miles. House on left behind sage green gates.

Susan Thorbek
Church Cove, The Lizard TR12 7PQ
Tel 01326 290877
Web www.landewednackhouse.com

Hill House

Wake to the sight and sound of the sea. A nautical theme punctuates the décor of this cottage house with strong colours and ingenious use of space. Bedrooms are truly comfortable, the kitchen and dining-room large enough to cope with small feasts, and the big living room ends in a little deck from which there are long, lazy views to the sea and, sometimes, the Lizard. The garden rolls past the summer house to a stream, then it's a short walk to popular Kennack Sands. Few other houses share the peace of this country lane, but there is a sense of community, and the caretaker lives nearby. Wonderful.

Price	£416-£900 per week.
Rooms	House for 4 (1 double, 1 twin; bath & shower rooms).
Meals	Restaurants/pubs within 20-minute walk.
Closed	Rarely.
Directions	Directions given on booking.

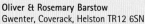

Oliver & Rosemary Barstow
Gwenter, Coverack, Helston TR12 6SN
Tel 01225 428854
Web www.adtel.co.uk

Treleague

Surrounded by the unspoilt coves and fishing villages of the Lizard, this simply converted 17th-century barn is home to swallows, who sometimes swoop in looking for their old nesting spot. The original barn doors on the top floor open onto a Spanish parador feel and a huge dining/sitting hall with wood-burner, handsome pine furniture and a large oil painting by Bart O'Farrel. Bedrooms are uncluttered and light with beams, iron beds and smart TVs; two are reached over a little footbridge. Mark and Carrie are warmly enthusiastic and give you good coffee, delicious fruit salad, and eggs from their hens.

Price	£64-£74. Singles £45-£55.
Rooms	3 doubles.
Meals	Pubs within walking distance.
Closed	Never.
Directions	A3083 Helston-Lizard. Pass HMS Culdrose airbase on left; at mini r'bout, left onto B3293 St Keverne; through Laddenvean; sharp bend towards Porthhallow; 250 yds on left, house signed.

Mark & Carrie Hayes
St Keverne, Helston TR12 6PQ

Tel	01326 281500
Web	www.treleague.co.uk

The Hen House

Greenies will explode with delight: Sandy and Gary are passionately committed to sustainability. Unless you're interested in recycling, a greeting talk with maps, loads of local tips and all things green, this isn't for you. More enlightened souls will adore the spacious, colourful rooms, the bright fabrics, the wildflower meadow with inviting sun loungers, the pond, the tai chi, the fairy-lit courtyard at night, the scrumptious local food, the birdsong. There's even a sanctuary room for reiki and reflexology set deep into the earth. Join in or flounder. *Minimum stay two nights. Children over 12 welcome.*

Price	£65-£75. Singles £60.
Rooms	2 doubles.
Meals	Pub/restaurant 1 mile.
Closed	Rarely.
Directions	Off B3293 to St Keverne from Helston, left to Newtown-in-St Martin. After 2 miles right at T-junc. Follow road for 2-3 miles then left fork. Round 7 bends then right at triangulation stone for Tregarne.

Sandy & Gary Pulfrey
Tregarne, Manaccan, Helston TR12 6EW

Tel 01326 280236
Web www.thehenhouse-cornwall.co.uk

Trelowarren

Deep in woodland, a mile from any road, thirteen eco-cottages in one of Europe's top five botanical sites. Truly visionary Sir Ferrers is creating a natural paradise and aiming at self-sufficiency in food and fuel – reluctant self-caterers note: no need to cook *anything*! Paints are organic and high-spec showers and baths are fed with reclaimed rainwater. And for the sybarite… Heals' tables, leather sofas, Conran crockery, ash floors, superb beds and cotton linen. Children can explore a vaulted chamber or go with the gamekeeper on a dusk wildlife walk. Gorgeous for family gatherings.

Price	From £425 per week for 2.
Rooms	13 cottages: 8 for 6-8, 3 for 3-4, 1 for 4, 1 for 8-10.
Meals	Self-catering. Lunch £12.50. Dinner, 3 courses, £28.
Closed	Never.
Directions	From Helston, A3083 towards Culdrose; pass Culdrose & left on B3293 for about 1.5 miles. At top of hill 3rd exit (not Mawgan village), pass Garras school then left, signed.

Mrs Anne Coombes
Mawgan, Helston TR12 6AF
Tel 01326 221224
Web www.trelowarren.com

Tremayne House

A fine late Regency country house with a sweeping cantilevered staircase, intricate door surrounds, flagstone floors, shuttered windows and beautiful proportions which hides in the Helford River woods close to Tremayne Quay and Frenchman's Creek. Juliet is an interior designer and her skills are evident: the double and twin rooms are furnished in lavish country house style mixing textured chenilles with silks and checks, florals and chintzes. The garden suite is more contemporary but no less plush. Top quality beds, fabulous flowers, lobster dinners and friendly, interesting hosts.

Price	From £110. Singles from £80. Suite £120.
Rooms	3: 1 suite & kitchen; 1 double, 1 twin, each with separate bath/shower.
Meals	Dinner £30.
Closed	Christmas & New Year.
Directions	A3083 from Helston. B3293 for St Keverne. After 1.5 miles left thro' Mawgan to St Martin. Past school left for Mudgeon, on to x-roads. Left & after 200 yds, right. At end of lane thro' large granite gate piers.

Anthony & Juliet Hardman
St Martin-in-Meneage, Helston TR12 6DA

Tel 01326 231618
Web www.tremaynehouse.com

Glendurgan

In 1827 a thatched cottage stood where the light-filled family house now surveys the glen. The sixth generation – as accustomed as their ancestors to receiving guests – has mixed family furniture, books and paintings with modern touches (such as the pristine, Aga-driven kitchen). Caroline trained as a cook and her breakfasts draw on the best of local and homemade. Bedrooms have sensational south-facing views; Violet, next to the bathroom, and Magenta, a few yards down the corridor, are as your Edwardian aunt would have liked. No TV but a grand piano, and garden heaven on the doorstep.

Price	From £85. Singles from £70.
Rooms	2 twins sharing bathroom.
Meals	Pubs/restaurants within four miles.
Closed	Occasionally.
Directions	Brown sign to Glendurgan from Mawnan Smith. Ignore signed entrance to garden. Continue on for 200 yards. Take private entrance through white gate on left hand side.

Charles & Caroline Fox
Falmouth TR11 5JZ
Tel 01326 250326

Nansidwell Barn

The view from the barn is heart-stopping: fields tumble down to the sea; Falmouth and St Mawes sparkle in the distance. Open the pretty doors to a light, open-plan living area: white painted stone walls, exposed beams, wooden floors, comfy sofas, roses on a table. The kitchen is smart with cream-painted wooden units and granite work tops. After a day out, shower with local soaps then flop onto white linen-clad beds. The Barn has a double with its own shower, a twin and a separate, sparkling bathroom. And there's room for two more in a lovely annexe of the owners' house (let in conjunction with the Barn).

Price	Barn £285-£905. Cottage annexe £145-£450. Prices per week.
Rooms	Barn for 4: 1 double with shower; 1 twin; bath/shower room. Cottage annexe (sleeps 2): 1 double.
Meals	Restaurant/pub within 20-minute walk.
Closed	Never.
Directions	Directions given on booking.

Nigel & Carrie Gilmore
Mawnan, Falmouth TR11 5HU
Tel 01326 251122
Email gilmore@nandc.fsnet.co.uk

Carwinion

Tidy gardeners avaunt! The 14 acres at Carwinion are a natural, unmanicured Victorian valley garden with a superb collection of bamboos, ferns and other subtropical plants. The rambling manor has the faded grandeur and collections of oddities (corkscrews, penknives, magnifying glasses) that successive generations hand on. Your charmingly eccentric host introduces you to his ancestors, his antiques, his fine big old bedrooms – and Jane gives you "a breakfast to be reckoned with". The self-catering wing has a fenced garden to keep your children in and Carwinion dogs out. *NGS, Good Gardens Guide.*

Price	£80. Singles £45.
Rooms	3: 1 double, 2 twins/doubles.
Meals	Occasional dinner. Pub 400 yds.
Closed	Rarely.
Directions	Left road in Mawnan Smith at Red Lion pub, onto Carwinion Road. 400 yds up hill on right, sign for Carwinion Garden.

Mr & Mrs A Rogers
Mawnan Smith, Falmouth TR11 5JA

Tel 01326 250258
Web www.carwinion.co.uk

Bosvathick

A huge old Cornish house that has been in Kate's family since 1760 along with all the pictures, books, heavy furniture, Indian rugs, ornate plasterwork, pianos and even a harp. Historians and garden lovers will be in their element: pass three Celtic crosses dating from the 7th century before the long drive finds the imposing house (all granite gate posts and lions) and a magnificent garden with grotto, lake, pasture and woodland. Bedrooms are traditional, full of books, antiques and lovely views; bathrooms are plain, functional and clean. Come then to experience a 'time warp' and Kate's good breakfasts.

Price	£60. Singles £45.
Rooms	2: 1 twin with separate bath; 1 twin with shared bath.
Meals	Packed lunch £4. Pubs 2 miles.
Closed	Easter, Christmas & New Year.
Directions	From Constantine, signs to Falmouth. 2.5 miles, pass Bosvathick Riding Stables, next entrance on left. Drive thro' gate posts & green gate. A map can be sent to visitors.

Kate & Stephen Tyrrell
Constantine, Falmouth TR11 5RD
Tel 01326 340103, 01326 340153
Web www.pasticcio.co.uk/bosvathick

Tregew Vean

Once the home of a packet skipper, this pretty Georgian slate-hung house stands in a sunny spot above Flushing. From the garden with its palms, agapanthus, olive and fig trees, you glimpse the Fal estuary. The house is fresh and elegant, with tenderly cared-for antiques and an entertaining straw hat collection in the hall; Sandra and Rodney – both chatty and charming – give you comfortable bedrooms in your own part of the house. Flushing is a ten-minute walk; there are two pubs that do food and a fish restaurant on the quay. There's plenty to do and you can catch the passenger ferry to Falmouth.

Price	From £80. Singles £45.
Rooms	2: 1 double, 1 double sharing bath (same party only).
Meals	Pubs/restaurants 0.25 miles.
Closed	Christmas.
Directions	From Penryn towards Mylor. After 1 mile right to Flushing. Entrance 1 mile down road on right, 30 yds before T-junction.

Sandra & Rodney Myers
Flushing, Falmouth TR11 5TF
Tel 01326 379462
Web www.tregewvean.co.uk

Tavern Rocks

Far from the chintz-cottage norm, in an unspoilt village. The kitchen is a triumph of modernity and in the cupboards wine coolers, lobster picks and coolbags for the beach await. Beyond the deep bay of the creamy living room the blue ocean stretches; the bookshelves are packed with interesting reads and there's a wide-screen TV. The master bedroom has sea views, huge mirrors and sisal floors; the others differ only in size. The showers are 'power', the floors heated, the towels thick and fragrant, the mosaics spotless. More bliss in the terraced garden, with a summer house and plenty of space to flop.

Price	£725-£3,300 per week.
Rooms	House for 6 (2 doubles, 1 double/twin; 2 baths, 1 shower).
Meals	Restaurants/pubs within 5-minute walk.
Closed	Rarely.
Directions	Directions given on booking.

Chris Clifford
St Mawes TR2 5DR

Tel 01865 452964
Web www.tavernrocks.com

Pelyn

Sheep on the hillside driveway remain curiously unmoved by the view that sweeps so lushly down to the creek. Set in its own green acres, minutes from golden beaches, this modern house built around an 11th century dwelling, is a peaceful, and contemporary hideaway. Smugglers from a nearby cove once visited; nowadays a tap at the door brings a lobster instead. Fresh flowers are some of the personal touches in light, airy bedrooms (one cosy with sofa) and charming country bathrooms. Tuck into home eggs and local bacon in the conservatory in summer as you gaze out on rabbits and birds.

Price	£75. Singles £50.
Rooms	2: 1 twin/double; 1 double with separate bathroom.
Meals	Lobster & wine dinner £30, by arrangement. Packed lunch £7.50. Pubs 5-minute drive.
Closed	Rarely.
Directions	To Gerrans & Portscatho. Thro' Gerrans, road to St Anthony Head. Just after Percuil, turning next drive right at 150 yds in dip in road & sharp bend. Signed.

Graham & Bridget Reid
Gerrans, Portscatho, Truro TR2 5ET
Tel 01872 580837
Web www.pelyncreek.com

Pelyn Creek Cottage

It's upside-down, so the open-plan living area gets the valley views; all is bright and neat inside. Upstairs: slate floors, checked curtains, navy sofas with stripy cushions; a log-burner for chillier times, an ornamental balcony if the sun shines. Bridget has thought of everything: a checked cloth, flowers from the garden, homemade jam and home-laid eggs. Creep down the narrow stairs: slate floors and a white bathroom suite shine in front of you, there's a cosy twin, and a double with king bed decked in green and white gingham. Open the stable door to your patio, bring out the barbecue.

Price	£425-£750 per week.
Rooms	Cottage for 4 (1 double, 1 twin/double; bathroom).
Meals	Pubs 0.5 miles.
Closed	Rarely.
Directions	To Gerrans & Portscatho. Thro' Gerrans, road to St Anthony Head. Just after Percuil, turning next drive right at 150 yds in dip in road & sharp bend. Signed.

Graham & Bridget Reid
Gerrans, Portscatho, Truro TR2 5ET

Tel 01872 580837
Web www.pelyncreek.com

Trevilla House

The sea and peninsula wrap around you – an enviable position – and the King Harry ferry gives you an easy reach into the glorious Roseland peninsula. Frog stencils add a humorous touch to the bathroom, and the bedrooms are old-fashioned and comfortable, the twin with garden views and a sofa, the double with sea views. Jinty is warm and welcoming and rustles up delicious breakfasts in the sunny conservatory that looks south over the sea. Trelissick Gardens and the Copeland China Collection are just next door, and the Maritime Museum, cycling, watersports and coastal walks close by.

Price	From £70. Singles by arrangement.
Rooms	3: 1 twin; 1 double with separate bath/shower & sitting room. Extra single for same party.
Meals	Restaurants/pubs 1-2 miles.
Closed	Christmas & New Year.
Directions	A390 to Truro; A39 to Falmouth. At double r'bout with garage, left off 2nd r'bout (B3289); pass pub on left; at x-roads, left (B3289); 200 yds on, fork right to Feock. On to T-junc., then left; 1st on right.

Jinty & Peter Copeland
Feock, Truro TR3 6QG

Tel 01872 862369
Web www.trevilla.com

Pollaughan Farm

Immerse yourself in the peace of the Roseland peninsula: here are long views over sheep-dotted acres, an idyllic beach and the coastal path minutes away. The cottages, and a Victorian wing of the house, have been beautifully restored by the environmentally committed owners and have an uncluttered, cosseting feel with open rafters, comfy sofas, contemporary fabrics, generous beds and spoiling bathrooms. Pretty gardens are child-friendly, you can play tennis, gaze at the wildlife pond and pat the donkeys; if you can't be bothered to cook, ask Valerie to whip up something local and delicious. Bliss.

Price	£300-£1,320 per week.
Rooms	Farmhouse wing for 5; 4 barns for 2-6.
Meals	Restaurants/pubs within 20-minute walk.
Closed	Never.
Directions	Directions given on booking.

Valerie Penny
Portscatho, Truro TR2 5EH

Tel 01872 580150
Web www.pollaughan.co.uk

Pine Cottage

The Cornish sea laps the steep quay of this narrow inlet's port, its blue horizon just visible from the window of the elegant bedroom high up on the coveside. A perfect spot to wake on a summer's morn. The house is as sunny as its owner, the guest bedroom charmingly informal with its hand-painted violet-strewn wallpaper, super big bed and shelves brimming with books. A handful of small open-top fishing boats slips out at dawn to bring back catches of crab and lobster. Clare will give you a splendid breakfast of warm fruit salad, local bacon and eggs and home-grown tomatoes.

Price	£85.
Rooms	1 double.
Meals	Pub 100 yds. Restaurants within 5 miles.
Closed	Rarely.
Directions	From Tregony, A3078 to St Mawes. After 2 miles, at garage, left to Portloe. Thro' village to Ship Inn. Right fork after pub car park. Cottage immed. on left between white gateposts up drive.

Clare Holdsworth
Portloe, Truro TR2 5RB

Tel 01872 501385
Web www.pine-cottage.net

The Lugger Hotel

A smugglers' inn dipping its toes in the cool waters of Portloe Cove; lobsters and crabs fresh from the sea offer scope for gluttony of the very best kind. The hotel is supremely cosy with a log fire in the snug sitting room, a couple of decked terraces for lunch in the sun, whitewashed walls, fabulous views and Wellington boots at the back door; order a picnic and spend a day on the top of wild cliffs. Fine bedrooms and bathrooms may not be huge, but all swim in seaside elegance and have super-comfy beds, power showers that knock you flat, bath robes, fresh flowers and flat-screen TVs. Bliss. *Minimum stay two nights at weekends in high season.*

Price	£160-£270. Suites & cottage £220-£370. Half-board from £105 p.p.
Rooms	22: 12 doubles, 7 twins/doubles, 2 suites, 1 cottage.
Meals	Lunch, 3 courses, £19.50. Dinner, 3 courses, £37.50.
Closed	Never.
Directions	West from St Austell on A390, then B3287 to Tregony. Left onto A3078 for St Mawes. After 2 miles fork left for Portloe; left at T-junc. In village.

Ben Young
Portloe, Truro TR2 5RD

Tel 01872 501322
Web www.luggerhotel.com

Hay Barton

The giant windows overlook many acres of farmland, well-stocked with South Devon cows and their calves. Jill and Blair give you locally sourced breakfast in the smart dining room with its giant flagstones and family antiques; later, retire to the guest sitting room with log fire. Bedrooms are pretty with fresh garden flowers, soft white linen, floral green walls and stripped floors. Gloriously large panelled bathrooms have roll top baths and are painted in soft, earthy colours. Guests are welcome to chuck a ball or two around the tennis court; there are good gardens to explore and restaurants nearby.

Price	£80. Singles £50.
Rooms	2 twins/doubles.
Meals	Pubs 1-2 miles.
Closed	Rarely.
Directions	A3078 from Tregony village towards St Mawes. After 1 mile, house on left, 100 yds down lane.

Jill & Blair Jobson
Tregony, Truro TR2 5TF

Tel 01872 530288
Web www.haybarton.com

Bosillion

A special set up. Beautiful rooms in your part of the house lead onto a pretty, tiered garden – take your breakfast out here and relax in the sun. Come for cool calm colours, elegant antiques, a big bedroom and a real sense of privacy. The farmhouse has been in the family since the 1600s and Annabel and Jonathon have renovated thoughtfully and with flair. Your delightful bathroom has everything you need and your fridge is filled with summer fruits, walnut bread, and local produce ready for your breakfast – continental only. You are close to Heligan, the Eden Project and the beaches of the Roseland peninsular. Wonderful.

Price	£80.
Rooms	1 suite for 2.
Meals	Restaurants nearby.
Closed	Christmas & New Year.
Directions	From Truro, A390 for St Austell. 6 miles on, through Grampound; on leaving village, at top of hill, right at speed limit sign into Bosillion Lane. House 150 yds on left.

Jonathon & Annabel Croggon
Bosillion Lane, Grampound, Truro TR2 4QY
Tel 01726 883327
Email jcroggon@tiscali.co.uk

Creed House

Lally and William have transformed a jungle into one of Cornwall's loveliest gardens, where secret paths tempt you into the woodland's dappled delights. Inside the lovely, big, rambling 1730s rectory, shimmering wooden floors are covered with Persian rugs and light pours into every elegant corner; large guest bedrooms are gloriously furnished with antiques. Breakfasts (feasts of organic and local produce) often turn into an early morning house party, such is Lally's sense of spontaneity and fun. You are in deep, tranquil countryside, and the Eden Project and Heligan are close.

Price	£94. Singles by arrangement.
Rooms	3: 1 twin/double; 2 twins/doubles, each with separate bath.
Meals	Pub/restaurant 1 mile.
Closed	Christmas & New Year.
Directions	From St Austell, A390 to Grampound. Just beyond clock tower, left into Creed Lane. After 1 mile left at grass triangle opp. church. House behind 2nd white gates on left.

Lally & William Croggon
Creed, Grampound, Truro TR2 4SL
Tel 01872 530372

Tregoose

Surrounded by a two-acre garden full of treasures (open to the public, by appointment and under the National Gardens Scheme), a classical late-Regency country house with a bit of eastern promise. Alison, charming and unstuffy, serves you tea in the drawing room where a Chinese cabinet graces one wall. In the dining room is a Malaysian inscribed silk-screen – a thank-you present from Empire days. Light, roomy bedrooms have elegance and style, super bathrooms and gorgeous garden views (over 50 varieties of snowdrop flower from November to March). The Eden Project and Heligan are nearby. *NGS, Cornwall Garden Society.*

Price	From £98.
Rooms	3: 1 twin, 1 four-poster; 1 double with separate bath.
Meals	Dinner from £28. BYO. Pub/restaurant 1 mile.
Closed	Christmas & Easter.
Directions	A30 for Truro, at Fraddon bypass left for Grampound Rd. After 5 miles, right onto A390 for Truro; 100 yds, right where double white lines end. Between reflector posts to house, 200 yds down lane.

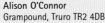

Alison O'Connor
Grampound, Truro TR2 4DB

Tel 01726 882460
Web www.tregoose.co.uk

Driftwood Hotel

The views are out of this world and Fiona and Paul are charming. Colours are restful, light pours in; there's a bar with comfy window seats and a lounge with handsome driftwood lamps, deep sofas, piles of books, a log fire. Food is brilliant, often from the sea, masterminded by a chef who has cooked in top London places; the restaurant is an expanse of white and wooden floor. Bedrooms, including four new, have fabulous linen and sea views from most, bathrooms are immaculate. Sit on the decked balcony for breakfast and drinks before dinner, or take a hamper to the private beach. *Minimum stay two nights at weekends.*

Price	£180-£220.
Rooms	15: 11 doubles, 3 twins, 1 cabin.
Meals	Dinner £39.
Closed	January.
Directions	From St Austell, A390 west. Left on B3287 for St Mawes; left at Tregony on A3078 for about 7 miles. Signed left down lane.

Paul & Fiona Robinson
Rosevine, Portscatho TR2 5EW

Tel 01872 580644
Web www.driftwoodhotel.co.uk

Bodrugan Barton

Everything's just right – the setting, the windy lanes, the gentle activity of the farm, the delightful hosts who look after you with such enthusiasm. What's more, there are freshly decorated bedrooms, good bathrooms, family antiques and the promise of a fine breakfast. The dining room is huge: even with sofas and a wood-burner, you could turn a cartwheel. An ancient lane leads to Colona Bay: small, secluded and full of rock pools. There's an indoor pool and sauna, too, and Heligan and the Eden Project nearby. Blissful. *Children over 12 welcome. Guided walks by arrangement.*

Price	£80. Singles £45.
Rooms	3: 1 double; 1 double, 1 twin, each with separate bath/shower.
Meals	Pub 0.5 miles.
Closed	Christmas & New Year.
Directions	St Austell B3273 for Mevagissey. At x-roads on hill, right to Heligan, avoiding Mevagissey. Through Gorran, bend left to Portmellon. After 1.5 miles, right at grass triangle into farm, before hill.

Sally & Tim Kendall
Mevagissey PL26 6PT

Tel 01726 842094
Web www.bodrugan.co.uk

Trevalsa Court Hotel

A big Edwardian country house with sprawling lawns that run down to high cliffs and steps leading down to a sandy beach. Mullioned window seats come in cushioned purple, flowers float in a bowl on the wood-burner and polished American oak sparkles in the panelled dining room. Bauhaus clocks and lamps add style, black-and-white photos adorn the walls, a bowl of lemons sits on an oak chest. In fine weather, sip drinks on the stone terrace or hide away with a good book in the summer house. Bedrooms are harmonious and varied, some big, others snug; all but two have sea views.

Price	£98-£150. Singles £65-£90. Suites £150-£200.
Rooms	11: 6 doubles, 2 twins, 1 single, 2 suites.
Meals	Dinner from £29.
Closed	December-January.
Directions	From St Austell, B3273, signed Mevagissey, for 5.5 miles past beach caravan park, then left at top of hill. Over mini-r'bout. Hotel on left, signed.

Klaus Wagner & Matthew Mainka
School Hill Road, Mevagissey PL26 6TH
Tel 01726 842468
Web www.trevalsa-hotel.co.uk

The Wagon House

Charles and Mally live *on* the estate of the Lost Gardens of Heligan! Where better for a botanical illustrator and a garden photographer to set up home? This is an 80-acre living museum of 19th-century horticulture: valleys, lakes, jungle, walled gardens, walkways. With the gardens and the coastal path right on your doorstep, you don't need your car; Charles and Mally will collect you from the station for free. There is comfortable furniture and light floods in through the huge windows. Bedrooms are simply decorated and the bathroom is spotless.

Price	£90. Singles £50.
Rooms	2: 1 twin with separate bath; 1 twin sharing bath (let to same party only).
Meals	Pub/restaurant 2 miles.
Closed	Christmas & New Year.
Directions	From St Austell for Heligan Gardens. Follow private drive towards Heligan House. Left before white gate-posts, keep left past cottages, left after The Magnolias and follow drive.

Charles & Mally Francis
Heligan Manor, St Ewe, St Austell PL26 6EW

Tel 01726 844505
Web www.thewagonhouse.com

Wisteria Lodge

Is it a small, elegant hotel or a posh B&B? The building is 70s modern in a small residential street and charming interior designer Sally has created a pampering space inside. Nothing is too much trouble: food can be cooked to order by the resident chef, beauty treatments and massages will be smoothly arranged, you can laze around the lush garden all day or leap in the hot tub – there are enough staff to pander to a small army. Bedrooms (some with whirlpool baths) are neatly dressed in saffrons, mustards and reds, mattresses are huge, towels are madly fluffy. Great for a house party.

Price	£90-£160.
Rooms	5: 3 doubles, 2 twins/doubles.
Meals	Light suppers from £7.
Closed	Rarely.
Directions	A390 2 miles east of St Austell, turning to Tregrehan opp. St Austell Garden Centre. First turning on left marked Boscundle Close, just off on right hand side.

Sally Wilkins
Boscundle, Tregrehan, St Austell PL25 3RJ
Tel 01726 810800
Web www.wisterialodgehotel.co.uk

The Old Quay House Hotel

A super little hotel with stylish bedrooms and seriously indulging bathrooms. Eight have balconies with glittering estuary views and flood with light, those further back look over Fowey's rooftops. Stop for a drink in the bar, then settle down to delicious modern European dishes in the 'Q' restaurant, smartly decorated in neutral tones, or spill out onto the terrace overlooking the estuary; you can breakfast here in the sun and watch the ferry chug past. Come for cobbled streets, a quaint harbour and enchanting Fowey – a great place to unwind. *Minimum stay two nights at weekends in high season.*

Price	£160-£220. Singles £130-£220. Suite £300.
Rooms	11: 5 doubles, 5 twins/doubles, 1 suite.
Meals	Lunch about £15. Dinner about £30.
Closed	Rarely.
Directions	Entering Fowey, follow one-way system past church. Hotel on right where road at narrowest point, next to Lloyds Bank. Nearest car park 800 yds.

Jane & Roy Carson
28 Fore Street, Fowey PL23 1AQ

Tel 01726 833302
Web www.theoldquayhouse.com

Marina Villa Hotel

The sun terrace at Marina Villa is bang on the estuary. Fishermen chug past, yachts head out to sea, gulls wheel and cry. The feel is Mediterranean – small, intimate, seriously elegant, with golden interiors, teardrop chandeliers, and housekeeping armed with dusters. Splash out on a fancy room; some big, some small, but all spotless and airy – hope for a sea view. You get rich fabrics, super art and swish bathrooms. Food is ambrosial, perhaps squab pigeon with espresso and orange, venison with chocolate and thyme, rhubarb sponge with stem ginger ice cream.

Price	£134-£174. Balcony rooms £184-£248. Singles from £90.
Rooms	18: 11 doubles, 2 twins, 4 balcony rooms, 1 suite.
Meals	Lunch from £17. Dinner, à la carte, £38-£45.
Closed	Rarely.
Directions	Down hill into Fowey; right (before bottom of hill) into Esplanade; on left. Ask hotel about parking.

James Coggan
Esplanade, Fowey PL23 1HY
Tel 01726 833315
Web www.themarinahotel.co.uk

The Cormorant Hotel

The road up is steep, but the reward is a breathtaking view of the River Fowey flowing through a wooded landscape. Boats tug on their moorings and birds glide lazily over the water; it is a very English paradise and as peaceful as can be. The Cormorant is very much a hotel – large windows and all those mod cons in the bedrooms – but it is run with massive family devotion and is superbly comfortable. There is even a great log fire. The heated pool has the best views and you can walk deep into the countryside from the door. Those views fill every room. *Children by arrangement.*

Price	£90-£160. Half-board £85-£105 p.p.
Rooms	14: 10 doubles, 4 twins.
Meals	Lunch from £5.50. Dinner, 4 courses, from £34.
Closed	Rarely.
Directions	A390 west towards St Austell, then B3269 to Fowey. After 4 miles, left to Golant. Into village, along quay, hotel signed right, up very steep hill.

Mary Tozer
Golant, Fowey PL23 1LL
Tel 01726 833426
Web www.cormoranthotel.co.uk

The Red & Blue Houses at Adventure Cornwall

Wonderfully rural, two newly converted farm buildings with beautiful, bright and minimalist interiors. The Blue House has a sunny Greek feel and is spacious with high ceilings, exposed beams, good sofas and a woodburning stove. The Red House has the same fresh contemporary design and a warm Moroccan feel. Each cottage has underfloor heating, a wet room shower, masses of outdoor space and a covered 'link' with long pine table – perfect for large reunions – and a magical yurt. Canoe, abseil, walk, then soak in the wooden hot tub. Your hosts are deeply committed to the environment but haven't forgotten to be fun.

Price	£350-£1463.
Rooms	Blue House for 6 + cot. Red House for 6 + cot. Yurt for 5.
Meals	Restaurants/pubs within 20-minute walk.
Closed	Never.
Directions	Directions given on booking.

David & Catherine Collin
Lombard Farm, Mixtow, Fowey PL23 1NA
Tel 01726 870844
Web www.adventurecornwall.co.uk

September Cottage

Your neat cottage is tricky to reach by car, so park at the top of the village and walk down the quiet lane. A scallop canopy crowns the doorway; pass through to cream walls, navy checked fabrics and country-smart furniture. Downstairs bedrooms have king-size beds; one has charming harbour views. The cabin-like kitchen is contemporary with granite worktops and smart appliances and has a dining area for two looking out to Readymoney Cove. Polruan has two pubs and a little tea shop, the twinkling lights of Fowey are five minutes away by ferry and the coastal path is 50 yards from the door.

Price	£235-£770 per week.
Rooms	Cottage for 4 (1 double, 1 twin/double; bath/shower).
Meals	Pubs within 20-minute walk.
Closed	Never.
Directions	Directions given on booking.

Christopher & Ann Walker
West Street, Polruan, Fowey PL23 1PL

Tel 01949 21125
Web www.septembercottagecornwall.co.uk

Collon Barton

Come for the lofty position on a grassy hillside, the phenomenal views over unspoiled countryside and the pretty creekside village of Lerryn. This 18th-century farmhouse is approached up a pretty, stone lane; it's a working sheep farm and an artistic household (sculptures galore) with traditional, peaceful bedrooms on the second floor and an elegant drawing room for guests. Anne sells huge dried hydrangeas and, on sunny days, welcomes you with tea in the summer house. Guided walks, canoeing and biking from the village and the Eden Project 20 minutes away. *Children & pets by arrangement.*

Price	£75-£80. Singles £45-£50.
Rooms	2: 1 twin/double, 1 twin.
Meals	Pub 10-minute walk.
Closed	Christmas.
Directions	A390 to Lostwithiel. Take 1st left down Grenville Road, signed Lerryn, 400 yds left at x-roads to Lerryn and St Winnow. In village, before bridge, left to Couch's Mill and Liskeard. 70 yds bear left into cul-de-sac and take farm lane 500 yds to top.

Anne & Iain Mackie
Lerryn, Lostwithiel PL22 0NX
Tel 01208 872908
Email i.mackie@btconnect.com

Pencalenick House

A design-junkie's dream: thrilling, elegant and secluded. Drift through a full-height sliding glass door into a living area with sweeping elm floor, magnificent stone fireplace, glass dining table, black leather chairs, soft-stone coloured sofas, stretches of bookshelves and masses of light. Perfect bedrooms have wooden shutters and creek views. The open kitchen has an Aga, espresso machine *and* a chef, keen to use local and organic produce; there's a wine collection for sampling on the decked terrace or private stony beach below, and a 47ft yacht with skipper to ferry you to secluded coves.

Price	£2,500 per day all-inclusive. Please call for information.
Rooms	House for up to 8 adults & 5 children (6 rooms: 4 doubles, 1 single, 1 bunk).
Meals	Restaurant/pub within 20-minute walk.
Closed	Rarely.
Directions	Directions given on booking.

Deborah Walker
Pont Pill, Lanteglos-by-Fowey, Polruan PL23 1NH

Tel 020 7747 6858
Web www.pencalenickhouse.com

The Well House

Silence in a blissful valley, with sprawling lawns, a swimming pool, a tennis court and lilies on the pond. There's a snug bar with busts and prints, a marble fireplace in the airy sitting room and a mirrored restaurant for fabulous food – perhaps confit of Gressingham duck, seared black bream with prawn risotto, hot coconut soufflé. Bedrooms are scattered about and come in a fresh country-house style: expect quilted bedcovers, sheets and blankets, warm colours and spotless bathrooms. You can head down to the sea at Polperro, take the ferry across to Fowey or drop in at the Eden Project.

Price	£145-£170. Suites £205. Singles from £130. Half-board £105-£135 p.p.
Rooms	9: 4 doubles, 2 twins, 3 suites.
Meals	Lunch, 3 courses, £23, by arrangement. Dinner, 4 courses, £37.50.
Closed	Rarely.
Directions	A38 to Liskeard, then B3254 south for Looe. Through St Keyne, then straight on down small lane at sharp right. House on left after half a mile.

Richard Farrow
St Keyne, Looe PL14 4RN

Tel	01579 342001
Web	www.wellhouse.co.uk

Buttervilla Farm

Gill and Robert are so good at growing vegetables (organically) they supply the local restaurants; all is cut and delivered within three hours. They're pretty good at looking after you too, in a totally relaxed fashion, with breakfasts of superb rare-breed bacon and modern Cornish suppers; fish and Red Ruby steak are specialities. No sitting room but bedrooms are big, colourful, comfortable and cared for; bathrooms are smart with solar-powered showers. Explore these 15 beautiful eco acres, stride the coastal path or head for the surf. Young and fun – with soul. *Minimum stay three nights July & August.*

Price	£75-£85. Singles from £55.
Rooms	3 doubles.
Meals	Dinner, 3 courses, £25. Restaurants 5-7 miles.
Closed	Rarely.
Directions	Turn by Halfway House at Polbathic for Downderry. House 400 yds up hill from inn, on left; signed before lane.

Gill & Robert Hocking
Polbathic, St Germans, Torpoint PL11 3EY

Tel 01503 230315
Web www.buttervilla.com

Sheviock Barton

This is Cornwall's 'Forgotten Corner' set in an Area of Outanding Natural Beauty. The house is opposite the church, rooted in time and space, its massive walls echoing their 400 years of history. All is fresh and delightful within, immaculate yet inviting. You breakfast in a perfect farmhouse kitchen: rugs on slate, Welsh dresser, comfy blue sofas and Aga to match. Heavy calico curtains and deep red walls in the guests' sitting room, bar billiards and table tennis in the games room, a charming simplicity in the warm bedrooms. Your hosts are the nicest people.

Price	From £70. Singles £40.
Rooms	3: 2 doubles, 1 family/twin for 3-4.
Meals	Pub/restaurant 0.5 miles.
Closed	Christmas & Boxing Day.
Directions	To Sheviock on A374. House opposite church.

Carol & Tony Johnson
Sheviock, Torpoint PL11 3EH

Tel 01503 230793
Web www.sheviockbarton.co.uk

Lantallack Farm

Life and art exist in happy communion: Nicky loves playing the piano and runs courses in landscape painting and sculpture. This is a heart-warming place – hens in the orchard, fine breakfasts in the walled garden, a super outdoor pool, a straw-yellow sitting room with a log fire... and bedrooms with delicious beds and books galore. The gorgeous old Georgian farmhouse has breathtaking views over countryside, streams and wooded valleys. Enjoy a hearty breakfast then set off to discover the Walkers' leat-side trail; you will be inspired.

Price	From £80. Singles by arrangement.
Rooms	2 doubles.
Meals	Pubs/restaurants 1 mile.
Closed	Rarely.
Directions	A38 through Saltash & on for 3 miles. At Landrake 2nd right at West Lane. After 1 mile, left at white cottage for Tideford. House 150 yds on, on right.

Nicky Walker
Landrake, Saltash PL12 5AE

Tel 01752 851281
Web www.lantallack.co.uk

East Penrest Barn, East Penrest Farm

A stunning stone and slate barn in a farmyard setting on the edge of the Tamar Valley. The barn's upside-down arrangement makes for a user-friendly space (and proper wheelchair access). On the ground floor, guests sleep in a row of cosy beamed, flagged bedrooms, each with a stable door to a sunny patio. Upstairs is breathtaking: a light-filled, 50ft-long, open-plan living area with a kitchen at one end and a book-filled snug at the other. Easy-going country antiques and rugs on pitch pine floors add to the charm – all topped off by the beautifully restored beamed ceiling. *Soil Association certified organic farm.*

Price	£400-£1,400 per week.
Rooms	Barn for 8 (4 doubles; 1bath, 2 shower rooms).
Meals	Home cooked meals by arrangement. Pub 10-minute walk.
Closed	Never.
Directions	Directions given on booking.

Jo & James Rider
Lezant, Launceston PL15 9NR

Tel 01579 370186
Web www.organicfarmholiday.co.uk

Hornacott

The garden, in its lovely valley setting, has seats in little corners poised to catch the evening sun – perfect for a pre-dinner drink. The peaceful house is named after the hill and you have a private entrance to your wonderfully fresh and airy suite: a room with twin beds plus a large, square, high sitting room with windows that look down onto the wooded valley. With CD player, music, chocolates and magazines you'll feel beautifully self-contained. Jos, a kitchen designer, and Mary-Anne clearly enjoy having guests, and give you fresh local produce and free-range eggs for breakfast.

Price	From £76. Singles £45.
Rooms	1 suite. Single room for child available.
Meals	Dinner, 3 courses, £18. BYO.
Closed	Christmas.
Directions	B3254 Launceston-Liskeard. Through South Petherwin, down steep hill, last left before little bridge. House 1st on left.

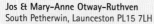

Jos & Mary-Anne Otway-Ruthven
South Petherwin, Launceston PL15 7LH

Tel 01566 782461
Web www.hornacott.co.uk

Trevadlock Manor

No wonder Mickey has a twinkling smile and Carey is relaxed and chatty – they're London escapees! And have landed here, in a house that dates from 1530 with a Celtic Cross and mullion windows. Light pours into the long drawing room with open fire, comfy sofas with bright throws, well-thumbed books and good pictures. Bedrooms (delightfully private in the west wing) are light, fresh and simple, with sleigh beds, hand-painted French furniture and glorious views; warm bathrooms have soft towels. A sizzling full English is all you need for tackling the moor – or a potter outside to meet the goats.

Price	£50-£70.
Rooms	3: 1 double; 2 twins sharing bath.
Meals	Light suppers available.
Closed	End July to end August & Christmas.
Directions	A30 to Cornwall. 6 miles beyond Launceston exit left to Callington on B3257. Through Plusha turn right to Trevadlock, North Hill. Follow lane for 0.75 miles, house on right signed.

Mickey & Carey Bruton
Lewannick, Launceston PL15 7PW
Tel 01566 782227
Web www.trevadlockmanor.co.uk

Trevadlock Manor Cottages

Five light, airy, old stone barns with a topsy-turvy layout: living areas are upstairs with neat kitchens, plump sofas, wood-burning stoves, fresh flowers; bedrooms downstairs with painted beds, white linen and a French feel. There are ornamental, or wooden sunny balconies and some have sheltered decks for outdoor eating. It's a short drive to the pub, but larger parties can arrange a meal in the manor. Mickey and Carey can tell you about the walking, sailing and riding. Such peace, yet you're close to Bodmin Moor, National Trust properties and the fabulous north and south coast beaches are reachable by car.

Price	£220-£800 per week.
Rooms	5 cottages for 4-6.
Meals	Pub 1.5 miles.
Closed	Never.
Directions	Directions given on booking.

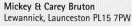

Mickey & Carey Bruton
Lewannick, Launceston PL15 7PW

Tel 01566 782227
Web www.trevadlockmanor.co.uk

Special Places to Stay series

Have you enjoyed this book? Why not try one of the others in the Special Places to Stay series and get 35% discount on the RRP *

British Bed & Breakfast (Ed 12)	RRP £14.99	Offer price £9.75
British Bed & Breakfast for Garden Lovers (Ed 4)	RRP £14.99	Offer price £9.75
British Hotels & Inns (Ed 9)	RRP £14.99	Offer price £9.75
Pubs & Inns of England & Wales (Ed 5)	RRP £14.99	Offer price £9.75
Devon & Cornwall (Ed 1)	RRP £11.99	Offer price £7.80
Ireland (Ed 6)	RRP £12.99	Offer price £8.45
French Bed & Breakfast (Ed 10)	RRP £15.99	Offer price £10.40
French Holiday Homes (Ed 4)	RRP £14.99	Offer price £9.75
French Hotels & Châteaux (Ed 5)	RRP £14.99	Offer price £9.75
Paris Hotels (Ed 6)	RRP £10.99	Offer price £7.15
Italy (Ed 5)	RRP £14.99	Offer price £9.75
Spain (Ed 7)	RRP £14.99	Offer price £9.75
Portugal (Ed 4)	RRP £11.99	Offer price £7.80
Croatia (Ed 1)	RRP £11.99	Offer price £7.80
Greece (Ed 1)	RRP £11.99	Offer price £7.80
Turkey (Ed 1)	RRP £11.99	Offer price £7.80
Morocco (Ed 2)	RRP £11.99	Offer price £7.80
India (Ed 2)	RRP £11.99	Offer price £7.80
Green Places to Stay (Ed 1)	RRP £13.99	Offer price £9.10
Go Slow England (Ed 1)	RRP £20.00	Offer price £13.00

*postage and packing is added to each order

To order at the Reader's Discount price simply phone 01275 395431 and quote 'Reader Discount DCN'

If you have any comments on entries in this guide, please tell us. If you have a favourite place or a new discovery, please let us know about it. You can return this form to DCN, Sawday's, The Old Farmyard, Yanley Lane, Long Ashton, Bristol BS41 9LR, UK or visit www.sawdays.co.uk.

Existing entry

Property name: ______________________

Entry number: ______________ Date of visit: ______________

New recommendation

Property name: ______________________

Address: ______________________

Tel/Email/Website: ______________________

Your comments

What did you like (or dislike) about this place? Were the people friendly? What was the location like? What sort of food did they serve?

____

____

____

Your details

Name: ______________________

Address: ______________________

______________ Postcode: ______________

Tel: ______________ Email: ______________

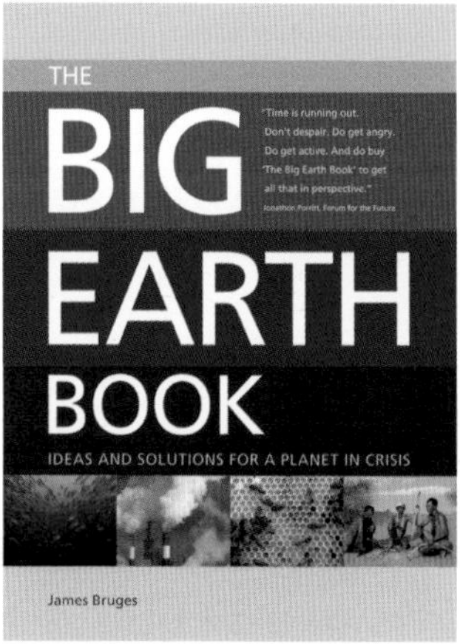

Praise for *The Big Earth Book*:

"Time is running out. Don't despair. Do get angry. Do get active. And do buy *The Big Earth Book* to get all that in perspective."
Jonathon Porritt, *Forum for the Future*

"This is a wonderful book – really informative but written in a very clear, easy-to-read way."
Patrick Holden, *The Soil Association*

We all know the Earth is in crisis. We should know that it is big enough to sustain us if we can only mobilise politicians and economists to change course now. Expanding on the ideas developed in The Little Earth Book, this book explores environmental, economic and social ideas to save our planet. It helps us understand what is happening to the planet today, exposes the actions of corporations and the lack of action of governments, weighs up new technologies, and champions innovative and viable solutions. Tackling a huge range of subjects – it has the potential to become the seminal reference book on the state of the planet – it's the one and only environmental book you really need.

James Bruges's *The Little Earth Book* has sold over 40,000 copies and has been translated into nine languages.

RRP £25.00 To order at the Reader's Discount price of £15 (plus p&p) call 01275 395431 and quote 'Reader Discount BEB DCN'.

Wheelchair-accessible

At least one bedroom and bathroom accessible for wheelchair users. Phone for details.

Devon

14 • 16 • 28 • 30 • 39 • 41 • 57 • 64 • 76 • 77

Cornwall

89 • 93 • 94 • 95 • 126 • 135 • 139 • 147

WiFi

Wireless internet access available for guests

Devon

5 • 8 • 9 • 10 • 14 • 16 • 28 • 30 • 39 • 40 • 41 • 45 • 46 • 47 • 48 • 50 • 51 • 54 • 56 • 57 • 64 • 65 • 70 • 72 • 77 • 79 • 87

Cornwall

104 • 105 • 108 • 111 • 112 • 114 • 116 • 119 • 120 • 121 • 122 • 123 • 124 • 126 • 129 • 134 • 135 • 147 • 148 • 149 • 150 • 154 • 156 • 158 • 159 • 161 • 162 • 163 • 166 • 167 • 168 • 169 • 171 • 173

National Cycle Network

These Special Places are within 2 miles of the NCN. (Route number in brackets. See www.sustrans.org.uk for details of routes.)

Devon

7 (2) • 8 (2) • 11 (2) • 12 (2) • 29 (2) • 30 (2) • 32 (2) • 33 (2) • 34 (2) • 35 (2) • 37 (2) • 39 (2) • 40 (2) • 44 (2) • 45 (2) • 48 (2) • 51 (2) • 57 (27) • 58 (27) • 59 (27) • 61 (27) • 62 (27) • 68 (3) • 74 (27) • 75 (27) • 77 (3) • 84 (3)

Cornwall

89 (3) • 90 (3) • 99 (3) • 100 (3) • 102 (32) • 104 (32) • 105 (32) • 106 (32) • 107 (3) • 108 (3) • 110 (3) • 111 (3) • 112 (3) • 120 (3) • 121 (3) • 122 (3) • 123 (3) • 124 (3) • 125 (3) • 146 (3) • 147 (3) • 148 (3) • 149 (3) • 150 (3) • 154 (3) • 155 (3) • 156 (3) • 157 (3) • 158 (3)

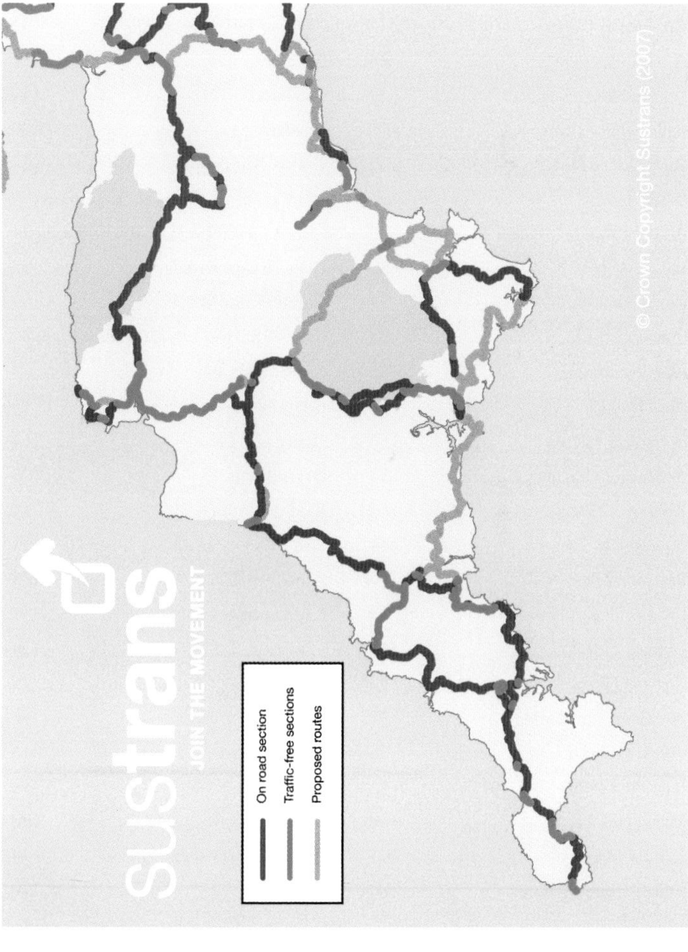
sustrans
JOIN THE MOVEMENT
On road section
Traffic-free sections
Proposed routes
© Crown Copyright Sustrans (2007)

11 Sea View Terrace	117
Applebarn Cottage	1
Avenue Cottage	33
Bagtor House	22
Ballaminers House	105
Bark House Hotel	67
Beach House	11
Beachborough Country House	76
Beachmodern No. 28	89
Beara Farmhouse	84
Bickley Mill	28
Blagdon Manor	86
Blue Hayes	116
Bodrugan Barton	155
Bosillion	151
Boskerris Hotel	112
Bosvathick	141
Bratton Mill	77
Broomhill Art Hotel	79
Browns Hotel	43
Browns Hotel	59
Buckland Tout-Saints	48
Burgh Island	54
Burnville House	61
Buttervilla Farm	168
Cabilla Manor	101
Calize Country House	107
Caradoc & Julian's House	95
Caradoc of Tregardock	94
Carmelin	131
Carwinion	140
Chydane	128
Collon Barton	165
Combe House Hotel & Restaurant	9
Corndonford Farm	24
Cornish Tipi Holidays	96
Creed House	152
Crooklets House & Crooklets View	90
Culm Valley Inn	3
Cyprian's Cot	15
Driftwood Hotel	154
Drym Farm	109
Easdon Cottage	19
East Penrest Barn	171
Ednovean Farm	125
End Cottage	35
Ennys	124
Fingals	39
Fingals Barn	40
Gidleigh Park	16
Glebe House	5
Glendurgan	138
Greenswood Farm	44
Halftides	130

Halzephron 129
Hay Barton 150
Hazelwood House 46
Heasley House 70
Hell Bay 126
Hewish Barton 78
Higher Eggbeer Farm 13
Higher Lank Farm 99
Higher Wiscombe 6
Hill House 133
Hillbrow House 80
Hooks Cottage 26
Hornacott 172
Horry Mill 83
House at Gwinear 110
Jamies 113
Kingston House 29
Kingston House Cottages 30
Knocklayd 42
Landewednack House 132
Lantallack Farm 170
Larkbeare Grange 10
Lavethan 100
Lewtrenchard Manor 63
Lower Coombe Royal,
The Garden Rooms & Coach House 47
Lower Hummacott 81
Lower Norton Farmhouse 37
Lydgate House 21
Manor Farm 31
Marina Villa Hotel 161
Molesworth Manor 104
Mother Ivey Cottage 106
Mount Tavy Cottage 58
Nansidwell Barn 139
Nonsuch House 41
Northcote Manor 82
Orchard Cottage 55
Organic Panda B&B & Gallery 115
Parliament House 32
Pelyn 144
Pelyn Creek Cottage 145
Pencalenick House 166
Penpark 25
Percy's Country Hotel 64
Pine Cottage 148
Pollaughan Farm 147
Polrode Mill Cottage 98
Porteath Barn 103
Primrose Valley Hotel 114
Rafters Barn 52
Regency House 2
Riverside House 34
Rose Cottage 7

Roskear 102
Sandy Park Inn 14
Sannacott 69
Sea View Villa 71
Seabreeze 51
September Cottage 164
Sheviock Barton 169
Shutters on the Harbour 118
Simcoe House 8
South Hooe Count House 56
Southcliffe Hall 74
St Vincent House & Restaurant 72
Staghound Cottages 68
Tavern Rocks 143
The Abbey Hotel 122
The Arundell Arms 87
The Barn, Easdon Cottage 20
The Cormorant Hotel 162
The Dartmoor Inn 62
The Devon Wine School 65
The Garden House 12
The Gardens 127
The Gate House 17
The Gurnard's Head 119
The Hen House 135
The Henley 53
The Horn of Plenty 57
The Lugger Hotel 149
The Old Coastguard Hotel 120
The Old Quay House Hotel 159
The Old Rectory, Martinhoe 73
The Old Rectory, Totnes 36
The Old Rectory, Widecombe 23
The Old Vicarage, Morwenstow 88
The Old Vicarage, St Ives 111
The Red & Blue Houses
at Adventure Cornwall 163
The Stables 85
The Summer House Restaurant 121
The Wagon House 157
The Well House 167
The White House 38
Tor Cottage 60
Tregew Vean 142
Treglisson 108
Tregoose 153
Treleague 134
Trelowarren 136
Tremayne House 137
Tremoren 97
Trevadlock Manor 173
Trevadlock Manor Cottages 174
Trevalsa Court Hotel 156
Trevilla House 146

Trezelah Farmhouse	123
Tudor House	27
Upper & Lower Tregudda	93
Upton Farm	91
Upton Farm Barn & Mill	92
Victoria House	75
Vogwell Cottage	18
Washbrook Barn	49
West Bradley	66
West Charleton Grange	50
West Colwell Farm	4
Wisteria Lodge	158
Woodside Cottage	45

Index by town

Ashburton	26-27
Ashwater	86
Axminster	1
Bampton	67
Barnstaple	76-79
Bideford	84-85
Bigbury-on-Sea	53-54
Bodmin	97-101
Bude	89-90
Budleigh Salterton	8
Camborne	109
Chagford	14-16
Chittlehamholt	80
Chulmleigh	83
Colyton	5-6
Crediton	65
Cullompton	2-3
Dartmouth	39-1, 43-45
Dittisham	38
Dulverton	68
Exeter	9-13
Falmouth	138-142
Fowey	159-164
Hayle	107-108
Helston	127-130, 133-137
Honiton	4
Isles of Scilly	126
Kingsbridge	46-52
Kingskerswell	28
Kingswear	42
Launceston	171-174
Lee	74
Lifton	87
Looe	167
Lostwithiel	165
Lynmouth	71
Lynton	72
Manaton	18-20
Martinhoe	73
Mevagissey	155-156
Modbury	55
Morwenstow	88
Mousehole	120
Newton Abbot	21-22, 24-25
North Bovey	17
North Molton	69-70
Okehampton	62-64
Padstow	104-106
Penzance	121-125
Polruan	166
Port Isaac	93-95
Portscatho	154
Saltash	170
Sidmouth	7

St Austell	157-158
St Ives	110-119
St Kew	96
St Mawes	143
Tavistock	57-61
The Lizard	131-132
Tiverton	66
Torpoint	168-169
Totnes	29-37
Trebarwith	91-92
Truro	144-153
Umberleigh	81-82
Wadebridge	102-103
Widecombe in the Moor	23
Woolacombe	75
Yelverton	56

1 B&B — 2 Cornwall

3 Buttervilla Farm

4 Gill and Robert are so good at growing vegetables (organically) they supply the local restaurants; all is cut and delivered within three hours. They're pretty good at looking after you too, in a totally relaxed fashion, with breakfasts of superb rare-breed bacon and modern Cornish suppers; fish and Red Ruby steak are specialities. No sitting room but bedrooms are big, colourful, comfortable and cared for; bathrooms are smart with solar-powered showers. Explore these 15 beautiful eco acres, stride the coastal path or head for the surf. Young and fun – with soul. *Minimum stay three nights July & August.*

5	Price	£75-£85. Singles from £55.
6	Rooms	3 doubles.
7	Meals	Dinner, 3 courses, £25. Restaurants 5-7 miles.
8	Closed	Rarely.
9	Directions	Turn by Halfway House at Polbathic for Downderry. House 400 yds up hill from inn, on left; signed before lane.

Gill & Robert Hocking
Polbathic, St Germans, Torpoint PL11 3EY

Tel 01503 230315
Web www.buttervilla.com

10

Entry 168 Map 2 11